Paper Creations
Cards and Gifts

Steve and Megumi Biddle

David and Charles

A DAVID & CHARLES BOOK
Copyright © David & Charles Limited 2005

David & Charles is an F+W Publications Inc. company
4700 East Galbraith Road
Cincinnati, OH 45236

First published in paperback in the USA by David & Charles in 2005
First published in hardback in the UK by David & Charles in 2006

Text and designs Copyright © Steve and Megumi Biddle 2005
Illustrations Copyright © Megumi Biddle 2005
Origami design folds Copyright © Steve and Megumi Biddle 2005
Photography Copyright © David & Charles Limited 2005

A catalogue record for this book is available from the British Library.

ISBN-13: 978-0-7153-2153-9 hardback
ISBN-10: 0-7153-2153-6 hardback

ISBN-13: 978-0-7153-2154-6 paperback
ISBN-10: 0-7153-2154-4 paperback

Printed in China by SNP Leefung
for David & Charles
Brunel House   Newton Abbot   Devon

Executive Editor Cheryl Brown
Editor Jennifer Proverbs
Art Editor Prudence Rogers
Production Controller Ros Napper
Project Editor Betsy Hosegood
Photography Ginette Chapman and Karl Adamson

Visit our website at www.davidandcharles.co.uk

David & Charles books are available from all good bookshops; alternatively you can contact our Orderline on 0870
9908222 or write to us at FREEPOST EX2 110, D&C Direct, Newton Abbot, TQ12 4ZZ (no stamp required UK mainland);
US customers call 800-289-0963 and Canadian customers call 800-840-5220.

Contents

Introduction

Using the simple paperfolding techniques demonstrated in this book you can devise unusual, attractive and surprisingly simple handmade gifts for friends and loved ones. Gifts made from paper and card won't cost a fortune but because they are beautifully hand crafted they are bound to be well received. There are 16 projects in this book for you to choose from, and each one introduces and applies a new technique, or builds on a previous one, so that by the time you have worked through the book you will be amazed at how easy it is to produce treasured keepsakes.

The projects have been designed for anyone who wants to achieve beautiful results quickly. By all means copy the designs as they appear, but what is important is your own touch – the feeling and life that you inject into your work. So feel free to adapt any project to suit the recipient or simply to experiment, which is the best way to discover new approaches and ideas. Enjoy the journey of creating something special for the important people in your life.

Using this book

We suggest that you work through this book from beginning to end, starting with the first section, which introduces you to the most versatile of materials – paper and card. Here we list the essential tools and materials you need to get started and explain the basic folding symbols. These are the backbone of paper crafting and will enable you to make the projects that follow. In this section we divulge a few secrets for folding and scoring paper correctly and we show how to make a template, two-panel card and a three-panel window card.

The second and largest section of the book contains step-by-step instructions

for making a wide range of delightful handmade gifts and embellishments for all occasions. Each project lists all the materials you need, with photographs and diagrams to help you achieve exquisite results. You'll also find a variety of ideas to help you adapt and personalize the projects and extend the range of possibilities. The projects are organized with the simplest or most fundamental techniques at the beginning. Some of the later sections are based on earlier ones, so we suggest that you work through them in order.

The final section of the book contains the templates you will need to complete some of the projects and includes a list of suppliers, which you may find useful when searching for appropriate tools and materials. (For information on using the templates, see page 15.)

We hope that our enthusiasm for all things paper will inspire you to make some of the illustrated projects and result in pleasure and satisfaction both for you, the creator, and the recipients of your gifts.

Steve and Megumi

A Lasting Gift
These fantastic paper tulips are just one example of the many exciting and inspiring designs in this book (see page 84).

Paper and Card

There are many different types of paper and card, varying from patterned to plain, textured to smooth. These can be found locally in stationery stores or at art and craft suppliers, or you can use a mail-order service or the Internet (see page 119 for a starting point in your hunt for resources). Here is some useful information to help you choose the right materials for your project.

It is all too easy to be seduced by the look of a paper or card, but if you have a particular project in mind you should check out its grain and be sure that the weight is suitable.

All papers and cards have a grain. If you fold with the grain you can produce a nice, sharp crease, but if you fold against it you may struggle to achieve good results and you are likely to produce a more uneven edge. To find the grain, lightly bend card both widthways and lengthways and see in which direction it moves easiest. It bends more readily along the grain.

Weight is a guide to a paper's other properties and to its price. In most countries, paper weight is given in grams per square metre and is abbreviated to 'gsm' or 'g/m²'. However, the United States uses pounds instead. As a general rule, lightweight paper is everyday stationery paper, such as photocopier paper, and weighs 80–120gsm; medium-weight paper is 120-150gsm; heavyweight paper is 150-250gsm and card is over 250gsm.

Paper that flakes or splits at the crease when folded will be unsuitable for the projects in this book. With card you can usually feel if it will be strong enough to stand up to a little wear and tear, or if it's going to buckle once it has been decorated. Always buy the best materials you can afford. Quality shows and, in the long run, it saves time, money and effort when used effectively.

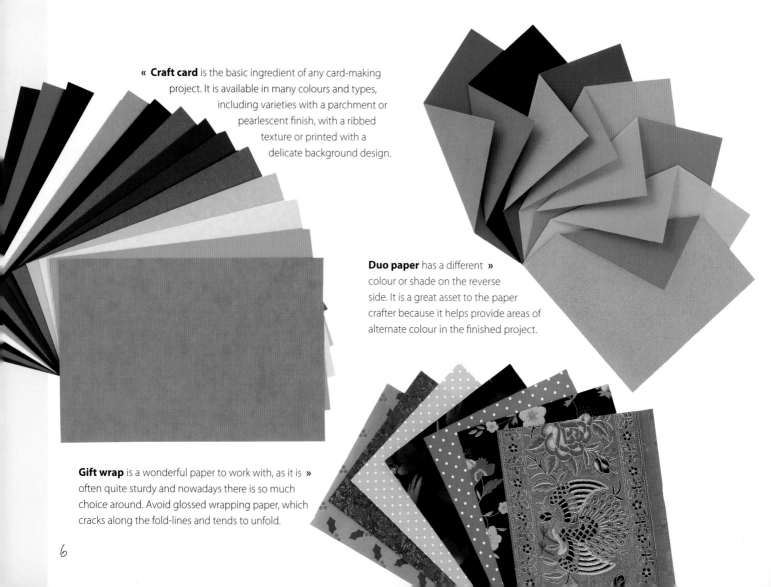

« **Craft card** is the basic ingredient of any card-making project. It is available in many colours and types, including varieties with a parchment or pearlescent finish, with a ribbed texture or printed with a delicate background design.

Duo paper has a different » colour or shade on the reverse side. It is a great asset to the paper crafter because it helps provide areas of alternate colour in the finished project.

Gift wrap is a wonderful paper to work with, as it is » often quite sturdy and nowadays there is so much choice around. Avoid glossed wrapping paper, which cracks along the fold-lines and tends to unfold.

« Handmade paper is often a softer and more fabric-like material than machine-made paper. Japanese washi and other handmade papers from around the world are left in a natural hue or given a solid colour, but much handmade paper is also made with exquisite designs and patterns, some so elegant they almost appear to resemble brocade.

Iris paper »
comprises strips of thin coloured paper. Gift wrap is ideal as long as it is not too thick because many layers are needed to make up the completed design. Patterned papers or those with abstract designs often work best.

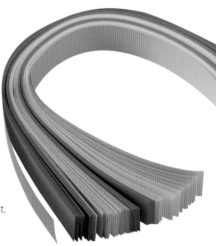

« Metallic foil, pearlescent and shiny papers are some of the more difficult materials to work with, but if you persevere the end results can look quite spectacular. They are readily available in rolls along with other gift wraps, especially in gold, silver, green and red at Christmas.

Origami paper   »
is most readily available with a solid colour on one side and white on the reverse. Most packets contain a rainbow of colours although occasionally you may find packets containing only one colour. This paper is available from specialist Asian gift shops, toy stores, and some stationery shops and art and craft suppliers.

Tea bag and kaleidoscope papers   »
can be obtained to make beautiful flower-like designs. Some sheets have just one design on them; others have two different but compatible designs. You can even cut squares from wrapping paper (as long as it has a repeat pattern) or, as in Hungary and the Netherlands, use the paper bag packaging that encases herbal and fruit teas.

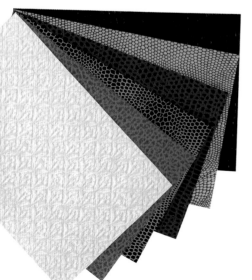

« Textured paper is available in a range of finishes, from smooth to rippled, wood grained and even with animal skin textures. It will make paper craft projects look extra special.

« Vellum paper is a translucent paper with a smooth finish. It comes in a variety of shades, patterns and embossed textures. Lighter weight vellum is easiest to cut, score and fold, whereas heavier vellum works better for projects that need greater durability.

Tools

It is a good plan to begin by assembling a basic tool kit because this is the equipment you will use again and again. The items listed here are found in our tool kit and were used for the projects in this book. You will need a few additional items for each project as well as the appropriate paper or card, and these are listed with the project instructions.

Felt-tip pen

Pencils

Eraser

White pencil

Red ballpoint pen

Self-healing cutting mat

Ruler

Tracing paper

Bone folder

Craft knife

Pliers

Scissors

Tweezers

Black felt-tip pen with a medium-sized tip is ideal for blocking in colour and for adding fine detail or drawing small motifs on a greetings card or gift tag.
Bone folder is a shaped tool that enables you to score and fold paper and card to give a crisp, professional finish.
Craft knife which is often easier to use than a pair of scissors when cutting long straight lines or intricate curves. The best and cheapest are those in which the blade is located within the body of the knife and sections are snapped off as they wear down. You could also use a scalpel. Store with care by retracting the blade if possible or sticking it into a cork. Replace blades regularly as a blunt blade will not cut cleanly.
Double-sided tape is sticky on both sides and is ideal for mounting card onto card and for sticking background papers and tea bag flowers to craft card. Cut it to length and stick it on like ordinary sticky tape, then remove the backing strip to reveal a second adhesive surface.
Eraser to remove guidelines. Choose one that will not leave marks on the paper or craft card.
Glue stick is a clean, quick and safe glue in a lipstick-type container. It is ideal for most light paperwork. Take care that the glue does not smudge the design on printed papers. Be sure to replace the lid immediately after use, otherwise the glue stick will dry up.
Hole punch for making holes in gift tags that can be threaded or to create decorative holes in paper.
Masking tape for holding paper and templates in position. It is low-tack so it can be removed without marking the surface.
Ruler for measuring and marking your material. If you also use it for cutting or scoring against, make sure you use a steel ruler or one with a metal edge. Always use a craft knife with a metal ruler – the

knife can cut nicks in a plastic one, making it unusable.
Pencils A 2B pencil is best for drawing and marking on your material because you can easily erase what you have drawn if you make a mistake. Use a white pencil to trace onto dark craft card.
Pliers/wire cutters for bending and cutting florists' wire to the required length.
PVA adhesive which is a safe, ready-mixed white solution adhesive that becomes invisible when dry. A small amount can be poured into a saucer or dish and applied with a cocktail stick for delicate work. If applied in large amounts to paper it will make it waterlogged and crinkled. When gluing thin materials together ensure the glue does not seep to the surface.
Red ballpoint pen is invaluable for transferring a traced template onto your craft material.
Scissors You will need a large pair for trimming and a small pair for intricate work. Cutting adhesive tape or glued paper can leave a residue on the blades that may then transfer onto your work, so keep the blades clean.
Self-healing cutting mat is the best surface for cutting on with a craft knife because the edges of the cut seal back up, or heal, so as not to leave an indent. The mat protects your working surface and has a resilience that makes cutting easier. However, the mat will only cope with vertical cuts – angled cuts will gouge out slithers or chunks.
Sticky tape is ideal for sticking paper and mending light objects.
Tracing paper is used to transfer templates onto your material (see page 15). Airmail paper or greaseproof (waxed) paper can also be used.
Tweezers can be useful for pressing small folds into place and for picking up and positioning small punched paper shapes.

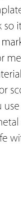

Glues

Embellishments

Embellishments enhance any paper-craft project and allow you to express individuality in your designs. There is a whole world of decorative bits and pieces out there waiting to be discovered, so keep on the look out wherever you go. Here are some of the items that we have found useful for adding that finishing touch.

« **Beads, charms and pompoms** come in an endless variety of colours, shapes, sizes and textures. They can be glued or sewn on, giving a theatrical feel to any project.

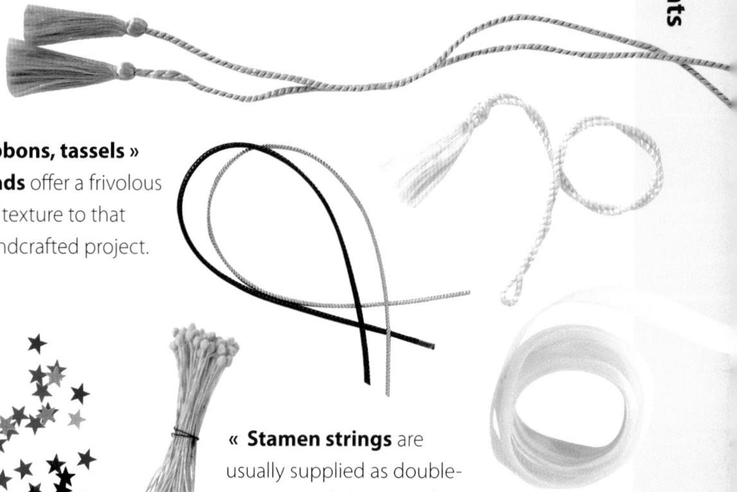

Cords, ribbons, tassels » and threads offer a frivolous change of texture to that special handcrafted project.

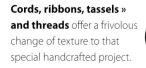

« **Craft stickers, » crystals, foilart flowers, gems, jewels and shiny stars** can usually be glued in place for added colour or sparkle.

« **Stamen strings** are usually supplied as double-headed strings that can be cut or folded in half. They are ideal for making flower centres.

« **Skeleton leaves** add texture and an unmistakably handmade quality.

« **Decorative paper punches** produce a hole and punched shape, either of which can be used in your projects. Hold the punch upside down so you can see where you are placing it.

Florists' wires » come in a large range of thicknesses (gauge). The wires can be bought covered with coloured paper. For the projects in this book use a 20-gauge wire.

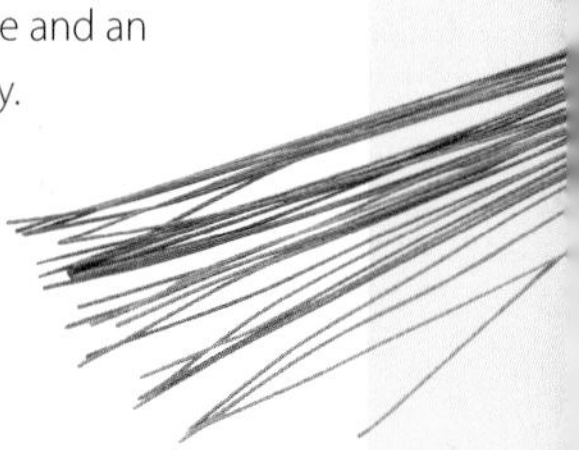

Deckle-edged » scissors, also know as paper edgers, can add interest to a finished greetings card. A light pencil line makes cutting accuracy easier.

« **Glitter glue** is fine glitter in glue. Use it directly from the squeezable bottle.

« **Floral tape** is from a crepe-like material, impregnated with adhesive. It is available in a large range of colours, including browns, greens and white.

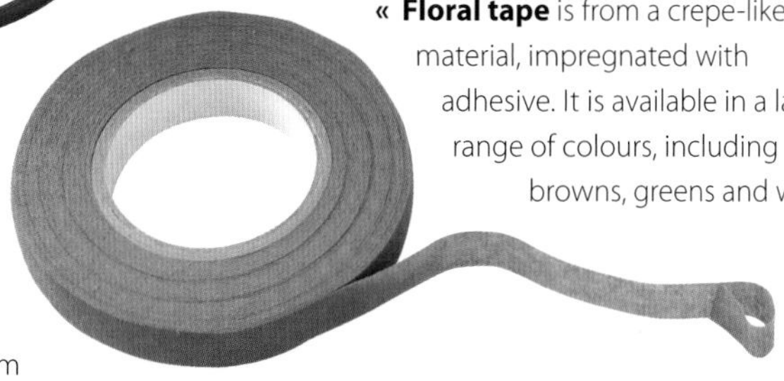

Raffia » is made from the leaf stems of a palm tree and is useful for making rustic-looking bows.

« **Adhesive foam pads** are small pads with adhesive on both sides. They raise whatever is fixed to them away from the surface for a three-dimensional effect.

« **Craft stickers (peel-offs)** come in as many different colours and designs as you can think of.

» **Oasis foam** is a plastic foam used as a base for dried and artificial floral arrangements. It comes in various shapes and sizes and can be cut easily with a craft knife.

Folding Symbols

The symbols that form the basis of the instructions in this book are used internationally. They show the direction in which the paper should be folded. If you are new to paper crafting, we suggest that you take a few squares of paper and study the following symbols and folding procedures before trying any of the projects. Look at the diagrams carefully to see which way the dashes, dots and arrows go over, through and under the paper/card, and fold your material accordingly.

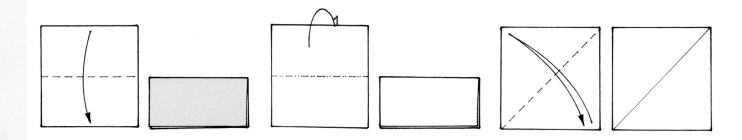

1 Valley fold Fold towards you or in front. This is shown in the diagrams by a line of dashes and a solid arrow showing the direction in which the paper has to be folded.

2 Mountain fold Fold away from you or behind. This is shown in the diagrams by a line of dots and dashes and a hollow-headed arrow. As in the valley fold, the arrow shows the direction in which the paper has to be folded.

3 Fold and unfold An arrow that comes back on itself means fold, press flat and unfold the paper back to its previous position, as shown.

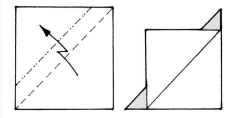
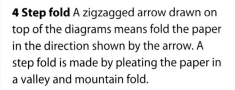
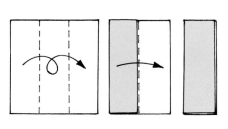
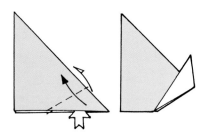

4 Step fold A zigzagged arrow drawn on top of the diagrams means fold the paper in the direction shown by the arrow. A step fold is made by pleating the paper in a valley and mountain fold.

5 Fold over and over A looped arrow drawn on top of the diagrams means keep folding the paper over in the direction shown by the arrow. Each fold-line represents one fold-over move.

6 Outside reverse fold Solid and hollow-headed arrows, and valley and mountain fold-lines instruct you to separate the layers of paper, taking one to the front and one to the back.

Helpful Tips

✓ If you find a special paper that you really like, buy several sheets and remember to make a note of the name of the shop or supplier. There is nothing more frustrating than finding that you only have a small corner of a particular paper left and not remembering where it came from.

✓ Avoid folding paper or cards that are coated on one side – they crack.

✓ Make sure that your working surface is level, smooth and uncluttered.

✓ Get yourself organized before you start a project. Have your basic tool kit ready (see page 8) plus any additional embellishments.

✓ Read through the project instructions carefully before you begin. In the diagrams in this book, the shading represents the coloured side of the paper. Look at each diagram carefully, read the instructions, then look at the next diagram to see what shape should be created when you have completed the step you are working on.

✓ Clean and clear away everything once you have finished the project in preparation for your next creative session.

✓ Above all, if a fold or whole projects fail to work out, do not give up hope. Go through the illustrations one by one, checking that you have read the instructions correctly and have not missed an important word or overlooked a symbol. If you are still unable to complete the project, put it to one side and come back to it another day with a fresh mind.

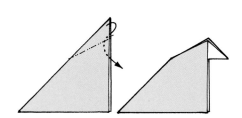

7 Inside reverse fold A wavy arrow with a broken tail and a mountain fold-line means push the point inside the model, in the direction indicated by the wavy arrow.

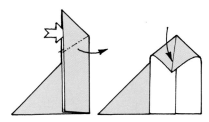

8 Open and squash A hollow arrow with a short, indented tail instructs you to open the layers of paper and squash them down neatly into the position shown in the following diagram.

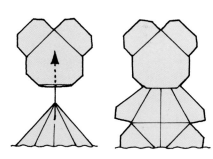

9 Insert An arrow with the tail broken near the head means insert the point into the pocket, as shown.

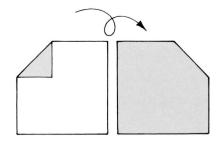

10 Turn over A looped arrow means turn the paper (or model) over in the direction shown by the arrow.

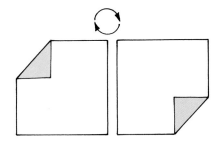

11 Turn around Two circling arrows means turn the paper (or model) around into the position shown.

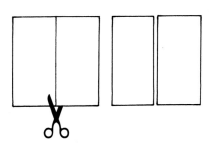

12 Cut A pair of scissors and a solid line means cut the paper. The solid line shows the position of the cut.

Folding

It is vital to fold paper neatly if you wish to become accomplished at paper crafting. There are many ways to do this, but this is the method we find works best. Here is how to fold paper for an insert, which can be in a colour to complement or contrast with the card.

Making a Paper Insert

You will need

✓ A4 (21 x 29.5cm / 8¼ x 11⅝in) sheet of paper
✓ Two-panel card
✓ Craft knife
✓ Cutting mat
✓ Metal ruler
✓ Glue stick

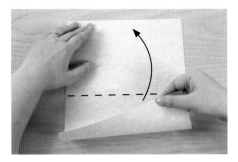

1 To fold, rest the sheet of craft paper lengthways on your working surface, so that an edge is near you. Hold down the paper's top edge. Lift the bottom edge and valley fold it up to meet the top edge.

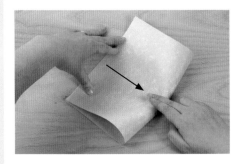

2 Keeping the edges together, run your forefinger down the paper's middle to the bottom edge to fix the middle of the fold.

3 To finish the fold, run your forefinger along the bottom edge to both sides, pressing the fold into place and checking the edges are still aligned.

4 Place the cutting mat on your working surface. Place the insert, with its folded edge on the left, onto the cutting mat. Using the craft knife and metal ruler, trim a 0.3cm (⅛in) wide strip of paper from the right-hand edges.

5 Apply a thin line of glue along the insert's folded edge, as shown.

6 Open out the two-panel card (see opposite). Place the insert on top, glued area uppermost and adjacent to the card's middle fold-line.

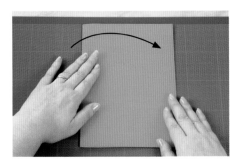

7 To finish, close the card from left to right and press firmly. Open out the card and the insert will unfold automatically.

Scoring

Making a Two-panel Card

Scoring card before folding it is vital if you are to achieve clean, crisp folds. Without scoring first a fold may have small creases along its length or it may not stay flat. So for neat, professional results, follow the instructions here, which explain how to make a two-panel card.

1 Place the cutting mat on your working surface. Turn the craft card sideways on and place it on the cutting mat. Using the metal ruler and pencil, measure and mark the middle points of the card's top and bottom edges.

2 Line up the metal ruler with the pencil marks and, being careful not to cut your fingers, draw the back of the craft knife across the card, adjacent to the ruler's edge, as shown.

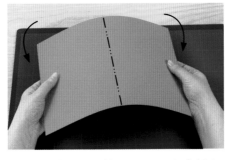

3 Along the scored line, mountain fold the card . . .

4 in half from side to side, aligning the edges, as shown in step 5.

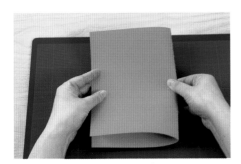

5 To finish, press the fold flat.

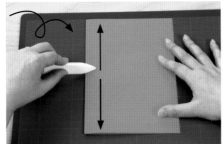

6 Turn the folded card from side to side, so that the folded edge is on the left. Use the bone folder on its side to press along the fold to make it sharp.

7 To finish, trim the card slightly if the edges are a little out of line.

Apertures

Making a Three-panel Window Card

As the title suggests, this card is made up of three panels, with a window in the centre panel that is ideal for displaying an insert. The side panels are folded over to cover the reverse of the insert.

You will need

✓ A4 (21 x 29.5cm / 8¼ x 11⅝in) sheet of craft card
✓ Cutting mat
✓ Craft knife
✓ Metal ruler
✓ 2B pencil

1 Place the cutting mat on your working surface. Turn the craft card lengthways on and place it on the cutting mat. Using the craft knife and metal ruler, cut it in half from top to bottom. Place one half aside as it is not required.

2 Turn the remaining half around so that it is sideways on. Using the metal ruler and pencil, measure and mark the top and bottom edges into three equal sections, as shown.

3 Line up the metal ruler with the left-hand pencil marks and use the craft knife to score across the card, as shown. Repeat with the right-hand pencil marks.

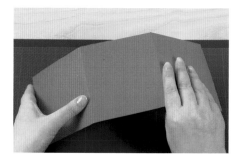

4 Neatly mountain fold the card into three panels along the scored lines. Press the panels flat.

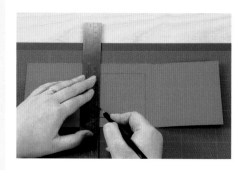

5 Turn the panels over from side to side. Open them out completely. Using the metal ruler and pencil, measure and mark a central square window on the middle panel, 7 x 7cm (2¾ x 2¾in).

6 Using the craft knife and metal ruler, neatly cut along the window's four sides. The middle section should fall away. If it does not, use the craft knife to cut the corners carefully so that it does fall away. Do not pull it out as you will tear or damage the corners.

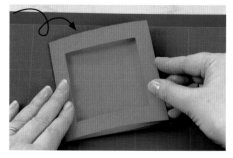

7 To finish, valley fold the panels over and over from left to right.

Templates

Transferring a Design

Some of the projects in this book require the use of templates, which you will find on pages 114–118. These templates are full size, but you will need to transfer them to your paper or card following the simple instructions here.

You will need
✓ Tracing paper
✓ Masking tape
✓ 2B Pencil
✓ Red ballpoint pen

1 Place a piece of tracing paper over the required template and, using small pieces of masking tape, hold it in place.

2 Use the pencil to draw carefully around the template.

3 Remove the masking tape and tracing paper from the template and turn the tracing over. Using the pencil, go over the back of the traced outline. If you want to trace onto dark card, use a white pencil.

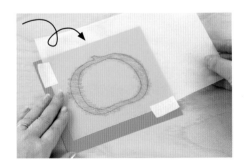

4 Turn the tracing paper back over. Reusing the pieces of masking tape, attach the tracing paper in the required position on your paper or card.

5 Using the red ballpoint pen, go around the traced outline again, pressing firmly to transfer the template.

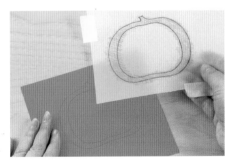

6 To finish, gently remove the masking tape and tracing paper.

Envelopes

Making an Envelope to Fit Your Card

You can buy envelopes in a variety of shapes and sizes, but by making your own you can give your gift that extra-special touch. You'll also be able to match cards that you have made in unusual sizes. Use quality paper to protect your creations if you are sending them by post.

You will need

✓ For a two-panel card: A3 (29.5 x 42cm / 11⅝ x 16½in) sheet of paper
✓ For a three-panel card: A4 (21 x 29.5cm / 8¼ x 11⅝in) sheet of paper
✓ Craft stickers

1 Depending on the size of your card, place the required sheet of paper length-ways on, with the white side on top. Valley fold the paper in half from side to side. Press flat and unfold.

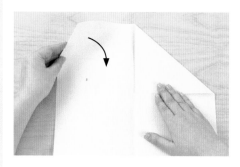

2 Valley fold the top corners down to meet the middle fold-line to make a shape that looks like the roof of a house.

3 Turn the panel card sideways on and place it centrally on the paper, adjacent to the 'roof'.

4 Valley fold the sides in and over the card, as shown.

5 Valley fold the bottom up and over the card, as shown.

6 Valley fold the top point down and over the card.

7 To finish, fasten the top point down with a craft sticker.

The Projects

Floral Easter Cards

Tea bag and kaleidoscope folding are very popular crafts in Europe, but they have very little to do with making items from soggy wet tea bags! In fact they are a form of origami using small decorative squares of paper, identically folded and glued together to create a circular pattern. There is an infinite number of ways in which a paper square can be folded and so there are many possible designs. The completed decorations look lovely on cards, tags or gift boxes.

There are four cards in this spring collection that would all be ideal gifts for Easter or Mother's Day. Every card features a different folded paper flower and each one is embellished in its own way. Although you can copy these cards exactly, we hope that you will also use them to fire your creativity. With this in mind all the cards are the same size so you can use some of the ideas for one card on another. You can also use different punches and trimmings to give your card a whole new look.

You will need

For the daffodil card

- ✓ Lavender two-panel card
- ✓ Nine 5cm (2in) squares of daffodil petal tea bag paper
- ✓ 10 x 15cm (4 x 6in) piece of pink pearlescent gift wrap
- ✓ 14 x 20cm (5½ x 8in) rectangle of sunshine yellow craft card
- ✓ 12 x 18cm (4¾ x 7in) rectangle of lavender craft card
- ✓ Blue sticky-backed gem
- ✓ Corner punch
- ✓ Butterfly punch
- ✓ Deckle-edged scissors
- ✓ Basic tool kit

You will need

For the yellow flower card

- ✓ Warm yellow two-panel card
- ✓ Eight 6cm (2⅜in) squares of cherry and butterfly origami paper for the flower
- ✓ 6 x 21cm (2⅜ x 8¼in) strip of bright yellow craft card
- ✓ 15cm (6in) square of bright yellow craft card
- ✓ Pack of white and gold peel-off strips
- ✓ Four gold craft butterflies
- ✓ Light blue sticky-backed gem
- ✓ Adhesive foam pads
- ✓ Basic tool kit

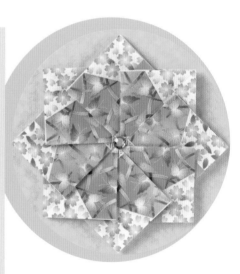

The two origami flowers shown on this page were made using tea bag folds. The daffodil flower (left) is 7.5cm (3in) across and the yellow flower (shown above) is 9cm (3½in) across. Two more flowers, which were made utilizing kaleidoscope folding, feature on the cards on pages 24–27.

Flower Fantasy »

These pretty flower cards are ideal for an Easter greeting, although they could be used for almost any occasion. They are deceptively easy to make, provided that you take the time to fold and crease accurately, but they will certainly impress your friends.

Daffodil Card

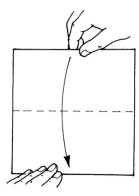

1 To make the flower, valley fold one square of tea bag paper in half from top to bottom, with the white side on top.

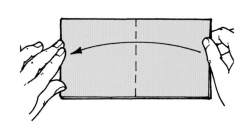

2 Valley fold in half from right to left.

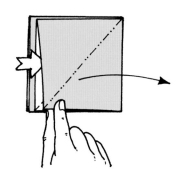

3 Lift the top half up along the middle fold-line.

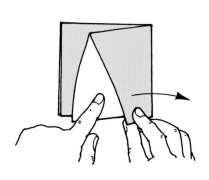

4 Open out the paper.

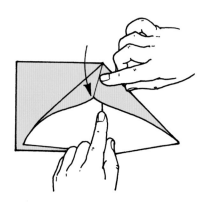

5 Push down, as shown.

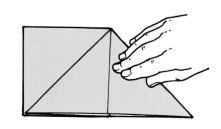

6 Press neatly in a triangle.

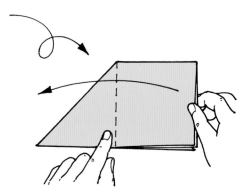

7 Turn the paper over. Repeat steps 2 to 6, making a waterbomb base.

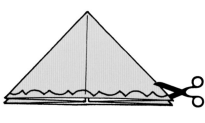

8 Using the deckle-edge scissors, trim along the base's bottom edge, as shown. Discard the lower part. Repeat steps 1 to 8 with seven further squares of tea bag paper.

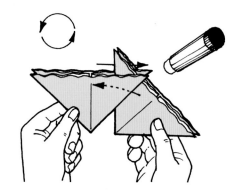

9 Turn two waterbomb bases around into the position shown. Slot one inside the other and glue them together.

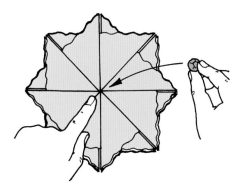

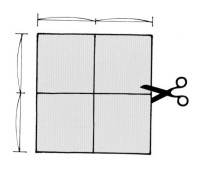

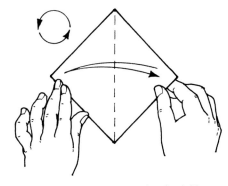

10 Keep on slotting and gluing waterbomb bases together to form a circular flower-like design. Remove the backing from the blue gem and attach it at the flower's centre.

11 To make the decorative units, cut the remaining square of tea bag paper into quarters. Place two squares aside as they are not required.

12 Turn one square around to look like a diamond, with the white side on top. Fold and unfold in half from right to left.

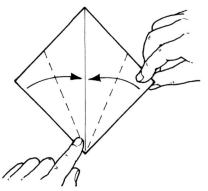

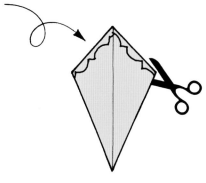

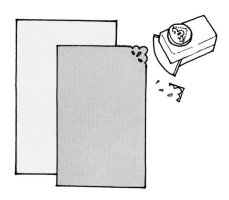

13 From the bottom point, valley fold the sloping edges in to meet the middle fold-line. Press them flat, making a kite base.

14 Turn the kite base over. Using the deckle-edged scissors, cut along the base's upper sloping edges, as shown, to make one decorative unit. Repeat steps 12 to 14 with the remaining square.

15 Turn the yellow and lavender craft cards lengthways on. Using the corner punch, punch all their corners. Apply glue to the back of the lavender card and mount it centrally on the yellow card.

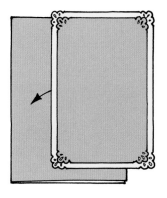

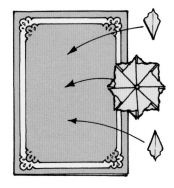

16 Apply glue to the back of the yellow card and mount it centrally on the front of the lavender two-panel card.

17 Apply glue to the back of the flower and mount it centrally on the lavender craft card. Glue the decorative units above and below the flower, as shown.

18 Using the butterfly punch, punch twelve butterflies from the pink pearlescent gift wrap.

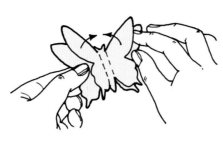

19 Glue two butterflies together along their middle lines only, with the coloured sides on top.

20 Lift up the upper set of wings slightly to finish one butterfly unit. Repeat steps 19 and 20 with the remaining punched-out butterflies to make five more units.

21 To finish, glue the butterfly units around the flower, as shown.

Yellow Flower Card

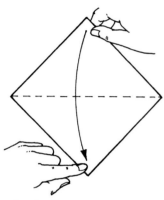

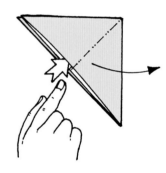

1 To make the flower, turn one square of origami paper around to look like a diamond, with the white side on top. Valley fold in half from top to bottom.

2 Valley fold in half from right to left.

3 Lift the top half up along the middle fold-line.

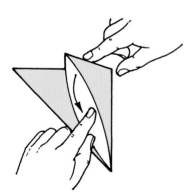

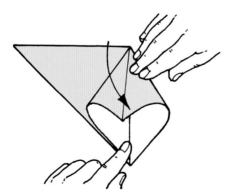

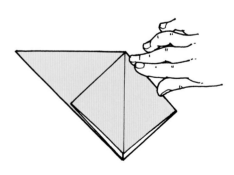

4 Open out the paper.

5 Push down, as shown.

6 Press neatly in a diamond shape.

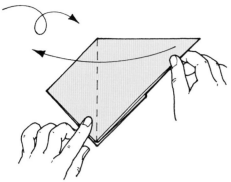

7 Turn the paper over. Repeat steps 2 to 6, making a preliminary fold.

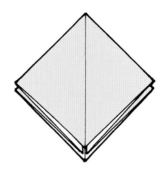

8 Repeat steps 1 to 7 with the remaining seven squares of origami paper.

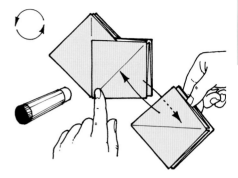

9 Turn the preliminary folds around into the position shown. Slot one inside the other and glue them together.

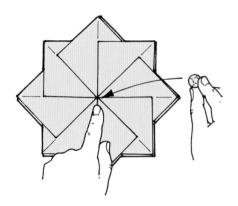

10 Keep on slotting and gluing preliminary folds together to form a circular flower-like design. Remove the backing from the light blue gem and attach it at the flower's centre.

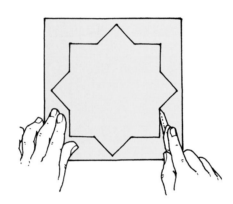

11 Trace and transfer the yellow flower's template from page 117 onto the square of bright yellow craft card. Using the craft knife, cutting mat and metal ruler, carefully cut around the solid black lines to make an eight-pointed star.

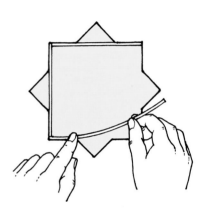

12 Attach white and gold peel-off strips along the star's sides, cutting off and discarding any excess. Make sure that they overlap each other, as shown in step 13.

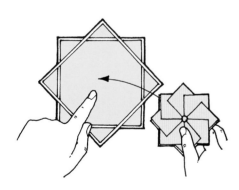

13 Apply glue to the back of the yellow flower and mount it centrally on the front of the star.

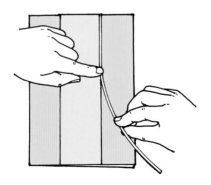

14 Apply glue to the back of the bright yellow card strip, turn it lengthways on and mount it centrally on the front of the warm yellow two-panel card. Attach two white and gold peel-off strips down the sides of the card strip, as shown.

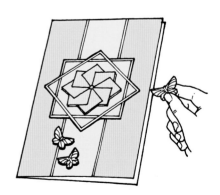

15 Apply glue to the back of the star and mount it centrally on the craft card. To finish, attach the gold butterflies on the panel card with adhesive foam pads.

Daisy Card

You will need

For the daisy card

✓ Green two-panel card

✓ Eight 5cm (2in) squares of green daisy tea bag paper for the flower and petals

✓ 13.5 x 17cm (5⅜ x 6¾in) piece of light green craft card

✓ Four laser-cut white daisies with yellow centres

✓ Purple sticky-backed gem

✓ Adhesive foam pads

✓ Basic tool kit

« Green Dream

The pretty flower at the centre of this card is 7.5cm (3in) across and utilizes kaleidoscope folding. It is made from pretty daisy tea bag paper and we continued the country theme by combining it with card in two shades of green and adding some pretty laser-cut daisies to the corners. The intricate cutwork on the pale green card is reminiscent of delicate garden trellis.

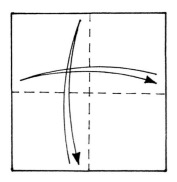

1 To make the flower, fold and unfold one square of tea bag paper in half from side to side and top to bottom, with the white side on top.

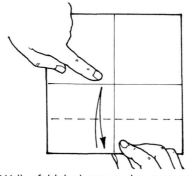

2 Valley fold the bottom edge up to meet the middle. Press flat and unfold.

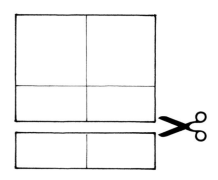

3 Cut along the fold-line made in step 2 to make a rectangle. Place the rectangle to one side, as it will be required later on.

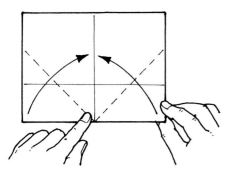

4 Take the larger piece and valley fold the right- and left-hand halves of the bottom edge up to meet the middle fold-line.

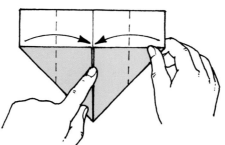

5 Valley fold the sides in to meet the middle fold-line.

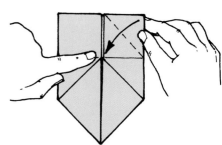

6 Valley fold the top right-hand corner down to meet the middle edges to finish one unit.

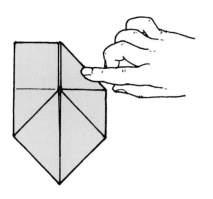

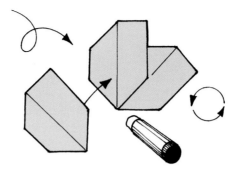

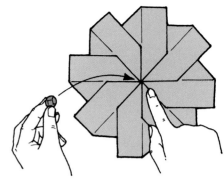

7 Repeat steps 1 to 6 with the remaining seven squares of tea bag paper.

8 Turn all the units over. Arrange them one on top of the other, as shown. The eight units will fit neatly together to form a circular flower-like design. Carefully glue them together.

9 Remove the backing from the purple gem and attach it at the flower's centre.

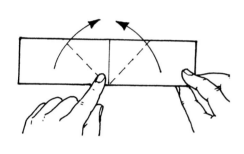

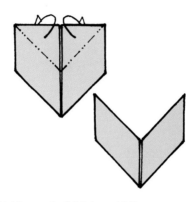

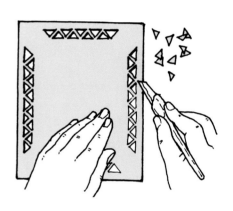

10 To make the petals, turn the rectangle from step 3 sideways on, with the white side on top. Valley fold the right- and left-hand halves of the bottom edge up to meet the middle fold-line.

11 Mountain fold the middle corners diagonally behind, as shown, to finish one petal. Repeat steps 10 and 11 with the remaining seven rectangles.

12 Trace and transfer the green daisy template from page 116 onto the light green craft card. Using the craft knife, cutting mat and metal ruler, carefully cut around the solid black lines to make a decorative border. Discard the triangles.

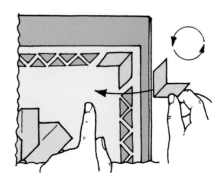

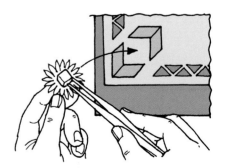

13 Apply glue to the back of the light green craft card, turn it lengthways on and mount it centrally on the front of the green two-panel card. Apply glue to the back of the daisy and mount it centrally on the light green craft card.

14 Glue on two petal units in the corners, one facing the other, as shown.

15 To finish, attach the laser-cut daisies between the petal units with adhesive foam pads.

Purple Flower Card

You will need

For the purple flower card

✓ Lilac two-panel card

✓ Two 5cm (2in) squares of harvest quilt tea bag paper for the flower

✓ 4cm (1⅝in) square of harvest quilt tea bag paper for the petals

✓ 7 x 21cm (2¾ x 8¼in) rectangle of purple flower-patterned vellum

✓ 7.5 x 21cm (3 x 8¼in) rectangle of pink pearlescent craft paper

✓ Purple sticky-backed gem

✓ Basic tool kit

« Colour Mix

The pretty flower on this card is made from a lovely tea bag paper using kaleidoscope folding. The overall effect is extremely complex, but in fact the background is made simply by layering two rectangles of paper on a two-panel card. The vellum on top allows the colours of the underlying paper to show through, producing a lovely, delicate effect.

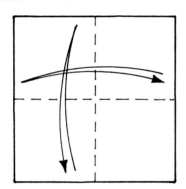

1 To make the flower, fold and unfold the two flower squares of tea bag paper in half from side to side and top to bottom, with their white sides on top.

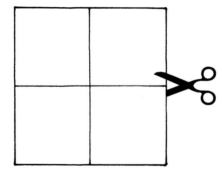

2 Cut along each of the squares' fold-lines to make a total of eight squares.

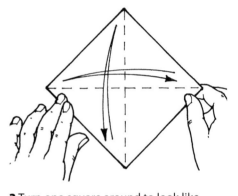

3 Turn one square around to look like a diamond, with the white side on top. Valley fold the opposite corners together in turn to mark the diagonal fold-lines, then open up again.

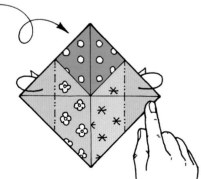

4 Turn the paper over. Mountain fold the right- and left-hand corners in to the middle.

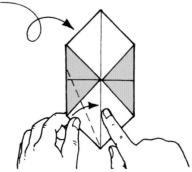

5 Turn the paper over. From the bottom point, valley fold the left-hand sloping edge in to meet the middle fold-line to finish one unit.

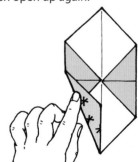

6 Repeat steps 3 to 5 with the remaining seven squares.

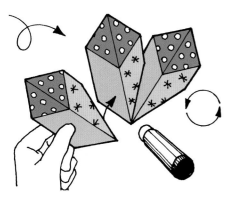

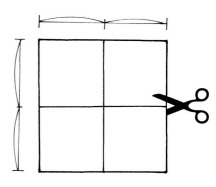

7 Turn all of the units over. Arrange them one on top of the other, as shown. The eight units will fit neatly together to form a circular flower-like design. Carefully glue them together.

8 Remove the backing from the purple gem and attach it at the flower's centre.

9 To make the petals, cut the petal's square of tea bag paper into quarters.

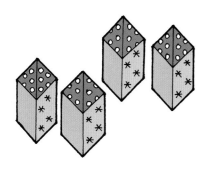

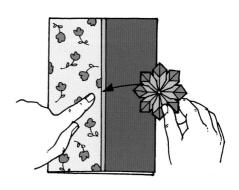

10 Repeat steps 3 and 4 with each square to make four petals.

11 Turn the vellum and pink pearlescent craft papers lengthways on. Apply glue to the back of both papers and mount them on the front of the lilac two-panel card, adjacent to the card's folded side, at the same time aligning their left-hand sides and edges.

12 Apply glue to the back of the purple flower and mount it centrally on the front of the two-panel card.

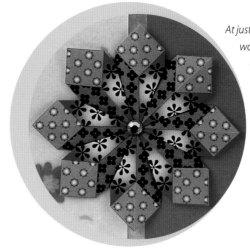

13 To finish, decorate the card by gluing on the petals, as shown.

At just 7cm (2¾in) across, this pretty flower would look wonderful on a gift tag or as an embellishment on a present, perhaps combined with some coordinating ribbon. The style of folding works particularly well with this tea bag paper, which is shown on page 7.

Handbag Gift Box

The anticipation of an unopened box has a special magic of its own, and an imaginative wrapping can add to the excitement; the fact that someone has taken the time to create a presentation box makes the gift all the more special. This handbag box will certainly impress a lady or young girl, and is suitable for any small items, such as a necklace or brooch.

You will need

✓ Square of patterned gift wrap for the box:
   small 25cm (9¾in)
   medium 35cm (13¾in)
   large 45cm (17¾in)

✓ Strip of matching gift wrap for the handle:
   small 2 x 15cm (¾ x 6in)
   medium 2.5 x 21cm (1 x 8¼in)
   large 3 x 27cm (1⁹⁄₁₆ x 10½in)

✓ Rectangle of coloured paper for the liner:
   small 5 x 15cm (2 x 6in)
   medium 7 x 21cm (2¾ x 8¼in)
   large 9 x 27cm (3½ x 10½in)

✓ Three-dimensional sticker to secure the lid

✓ Basic tool kit

Easy to make, this box can look extremely decorative when created from patterned gift wrap or handmade paper. Once the basic folding technique has been mastered many variations are possible. The instructions given apply to three sizes of box: small (5cm/2in square), medium (7cm/2¾in square), and large (9cm/3½in square).

As a finishing touch, use a three-dimensional sticker as the closure. You can buy some lovely versions ready-made or make your own by placing one sticker on top of another, or by adding sequins, beads, glitter glues or punched paper shapes.

Fashionably Feminine »

Small gifts are often the nicest ones, and you can make even more of them with the right form of presentation, like these super handbag boxes. The small and large boxes are shown in the main photograph. The medium box design is shown above; a three-dimensional sticker has been added to the handle for an extra-special finish.

28

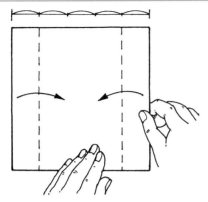

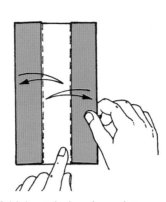

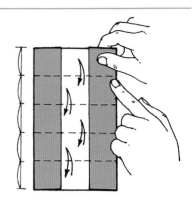

1 To make the box, use the pencil and ruler to divide the top and bottom edges of the box's square into five equal sections, with the white side on top. Valley fold one equal section on each side, as shown, to make panels.

2 Valley fold the right-hand panel, as shown. Press flat and unfold. Repeat with the left-hand panel.

3 Using the pencil and ruler, divide the panels into five equal sections, as shown. Using the pencil marks as a guide, valley fold each section. Press flat and unfold.

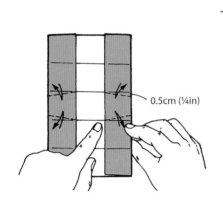

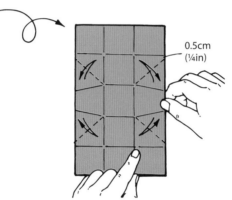

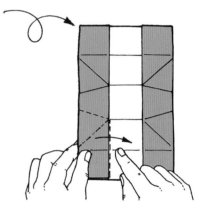

4 Treating the layers of paper as if they were one, make the valley folds shown, noting the 0.5cm (¼in) location points where the folds hit the panels' sides. Press flat and unfold.

5 Turn the paper over. Again, treating the layers of paper as one, make the valley folds, as shown, noting the 0.5cm (¼in) location points where the folds hit the panels' sides. Press flat and unfold.

6 Turn the paper over. Using the existing fold-lines shown on the left-hand panel, bring the top edge upwards, as shown in step 7.

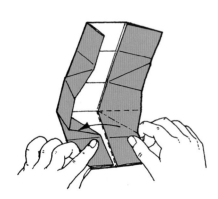

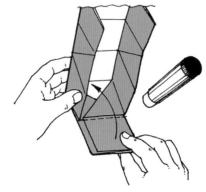

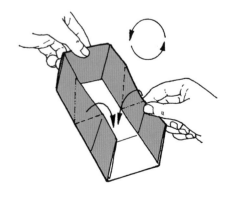

7 Again using the existing fold-lines, make the fold shown on the opposite side to bring the right edge over the left one and create a flap at the front.

8 Valley fold the flap into the box. Glue it down to lock all the folds together.

9 Turn the paper around so that the other end is facing you. Once again, use the existing fold-lines to create another flap.

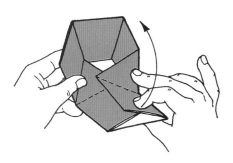

10 Valley fold the flap upright.

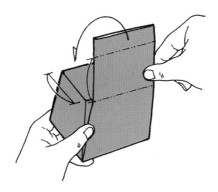

11 Make the two mountain folds on the flap, as shown, to create the box lid.

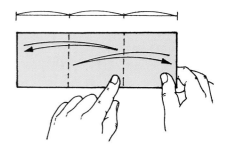

12 To make the liner, place the rectangle of paper sideways on. Divide into three across the width by valley folding and then open the folds so that the sides stand upright.

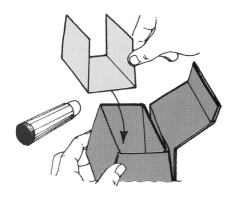

13 Apply glue around the outside of the liner and carefully insert it into the box, as shown. Press it firmly into place.

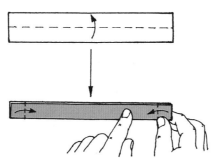

14 To make the handle, place the paper strip sideways on, with the white side on top. Valley fold it in half from bottom to top. Valley fold the sides over a little to make two tabs.

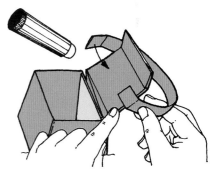

15 Glue the two tabs to the inside of the lid, as shown.

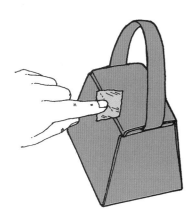

16 To finish, put your gift inside the box. Now insert the lid's flap into the box and hold it neatly in place with the three-dimensional sticker.

Luxurious Lining »
Being cube-shaped, the box can hold more than you might expect. Make it in a size a little larger than the gift for a snug fit, remembering to allow for any additional wrapping. The liner inside the box adds a sumptuous feel.

Wallet and Cardholder

This chic wallet and cardholder are perfect for a person who likes to travel light. The wallet is thoughtfully styled to fit neatly into the breast pocket of a shirt or jacket, and it has three internal pockets to keep your money safe. The cardholder keeps business or calling cards clean and fresh and can be styled to suit your taste or that of the recipient. These practical gifts are so desirable that you will probably want to make a set for yourself.

You will need

For the wallet

✓ 23 x 26cm (9¹⁄₁₆ x 10¼in) piece of copper-coloured gift wrap (plain on reverse)

✓ 26 x 42cm (10¼ x 16½in) piece of brown reptile skin gift wrap (plain on reverse)

For the cardholder

✓ A4 (21 x 29.5cm / 8¼ x 11⅝in) sheet of red leather gift wrap (plain on reverse)

✓ Basic tool kit

Made from gift wrap, these super accessories look like a million dollars but cost practically nothing to make. You'll need just two coordinating papers for the wallet and only one paper for the cardholder, so take your time choosing the right papers for an elegant finish. For the wallets we used reptile skin gift wrap with a coordinating metallic paper to emulate more expensive leather versions, but you could opt for a handmade paper with a coordinating plain paper or choose just about anything you like. You could even use duo paper, which has a colour on both sides. The finished wallet is 9 x 18cm (3½ x 7in) and the cardholder is 7 x 10cm (2¾ x 4in).

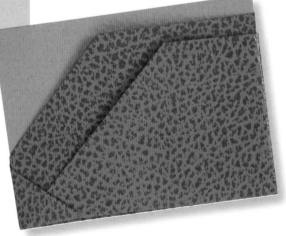

If you have a business or calling card, you'll know that a cardholder is an essential item to keep your cards looking their best. This version outshines the standard ones you can buy because its colourful, unusual and tailor-made. You can be sure that yours will stand out from the rest. Follow the instructions on pages 36–37 to make this cardholder.

Masculine Chic »

**Although made from paper, this wallet is surprisingly robust and should last well.
Simple to make, you may find yourself making one for every occasion!**

Wallet

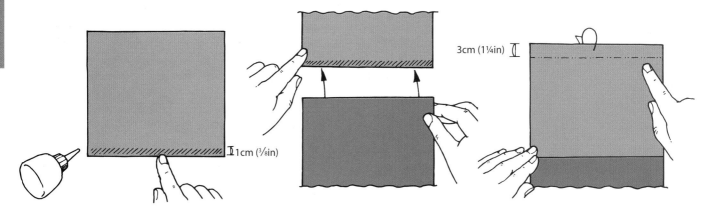

1 Place the piece of copper-coloured gift wrap sideways on, with the coloured side on top. Along the bottom edge apply a horizontal band of glue that is 1cm (³⁄₈in) wide, as shown.

2 Turn the piece of reptile skin gift wrap lengthways on, with the coloured side on top. Position it exactly over the band of glue, aligning the top edges and sides of both papers. Press firmly.

3 Mountain fold the top edge behind along a horizontal line that is 3cm (1¼in) away from the top edge.

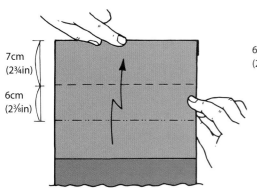

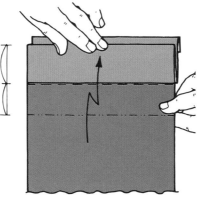

4 Valley fold the paper up along a horizontal line that is 7cm (2¾in) away from the top edge and mountain fold it down along a horizontal line that is 6cm (2³⁄₈in) away from the valley fold to pleat the paper.

5 Valley fold the paper up along a horizontal line that is 6cm (2³⁄₈in) away from the adjacent edge and mountain fold it down along a horizontal line that is 5cm (2in) away from the valley fold, again pleating the paper.

6 Press the paper flat.

The reptile skin gift wrap used for this wallet and for the grey variation shown opposite was a real find. We recommend that when you see a paper like this you buy two sheets, one to use and one to file with a note of the shop name in case you wish to buy it again. Look out for coordinating papers at the same time.

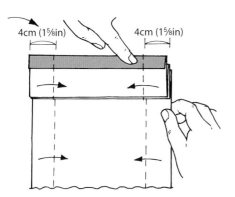

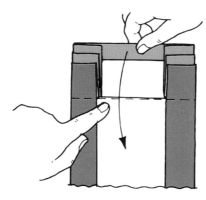

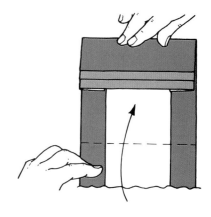

7 Turn the paper over. Valley fold the sides over, making two 4cm (1⅝in) wide bands of paper.

8 Treating all the layers of paper as if they were one, valley fold the top edge down along a horizontal line that runs adjacent to the pleats' bottom edge.

9 Valley fold the bottom edge up…

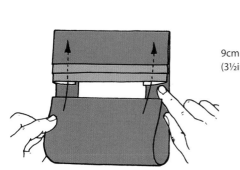

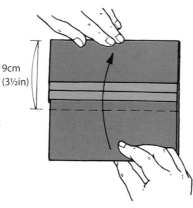

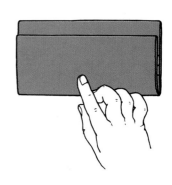

10 inserting it deep into the upper layers of paper.

11 Valley fold the bottom edge up along a horizontal line that is 9cm (3½in) down from the top edge.

12 To finish, press the paper flat.

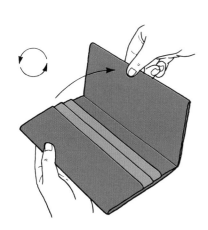

13 Open the wallet to reveal the three internal pockets.

Variation in Grey and Silver »
This wallet combines grey reptile skin paper with silver gift wrap for a classical look. However, there are many other variations you could try. Keep a look out wherever gift wrap is available because you never know what you might see that would work really well.

Cardholder

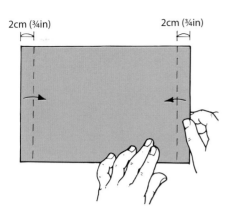
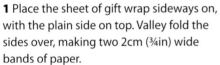

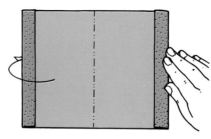

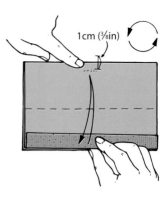

1 Place the sheet of gift wrap sideways on, with the plain side on top. Valley fold the sides over, making two 2cm (¾in) wide bands of paper.

2 Mountain fold in half from side to side.

3 Turn the paper around into the position shown. Valley fold the front flap of paper up to a point that is 1cm (⅜in) down from the top edge. Press flat and unfold.

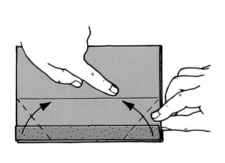

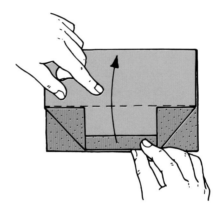

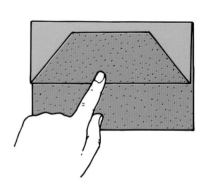

4 Valley fold the front flap's bottom corners up to meet the fold-line made in step 3.

5 Valley fold the front flap up along the fold-line made in step 3.

6 Press the paper flat.

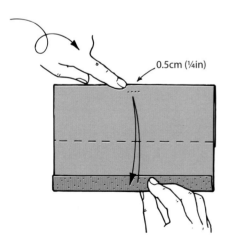

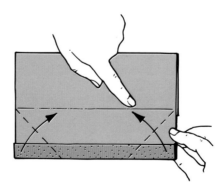

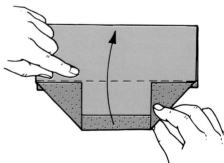

7 Turn the paper over. Valley fold the bottom edge up to a point that is 0.5cm (¼in) down from the top edge. Press flat and unfold.

8 Valley fold the bottom corners up to meet the fold-line made in step 7.

9 Valley fold the bottom edge up along the fold-line made in step 7.

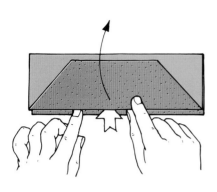

10 Open out the paper from bottom to top, as shown.

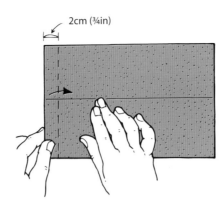

2cm (¾in)

11 Valley fold the left-hand side over, making a 2cm (¾in) wide band of paper.

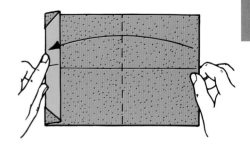

12 Valley fold the right-hand side over to the left, at the same time . . .

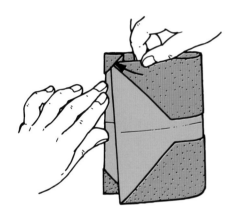

13 inserting its top corner into the adjacent left-hand triangular pocket.

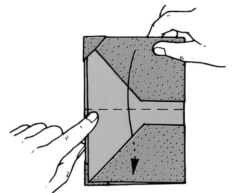

14 Valley fold in half from top to bottom, at the same time inserting the top edge deep into the lower pocket.

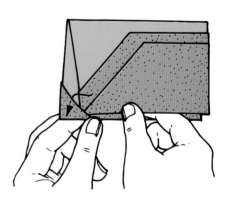

15 Insert the bottom left-hand corner into the adjacent triangular pocket.

16 Your business card can be inserted in the front pocket of the finished cardholder. There is also another pocket on the back.

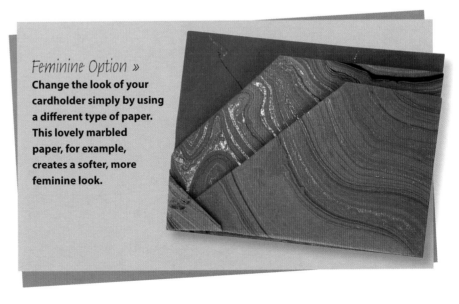

Feminine Option »
Change the look of your cardholder simply by using a different type of paper. This lovely marbled paper, for example, creates a softer, more feminine look.

37

Woven Heart Gift Basket

It is believed that Hans Christian Andersen, the Danish fairy-tale writer, first created the interwoven heart basket. Traditionally it is red and white, the colours of the Danish flag. Through the years, this intricate handmade item has come to symbolize romance, respect and good wishes. Filled with chocolates, flowers or a love note, it makes a charming Valentine for someone special.

You will need

For each heart basket

- ✓ 6 x 18cm (2⅜ x 7in) rectangle of red craft paper
- ✓ 6 x 18cm (2⅜ x 7in) rectangle of gold craft paper or the colour of your choice
- ✓ 1.2 x 18cm (½ x 7in) strip of red craft paper for the handle
- ✓ Basic tool kit

Paper weaving is fun and the results can look spectacular, as you can see here, when it looks as if the finished baskets are impossible. In fact, we are so sure that you are going to enjoy this technique that we have provided three weaving templates so you can choose your favourite or even make all three. The process is the same no matter which heart you decide to make, so just follow the instructions for the red and gold chequered heart and use your chosen template from page 118. There's also a Valentine card to make plus a stylish name or menu holder. The finished basket is 9.5cm (3¾in) high plus the handle and 10cm (4in) across, but you can make a larger version, if desired.

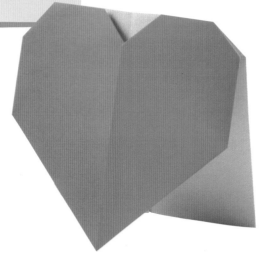

« Heart Holder

This pretty heart can be used to hold a place card or menu on the dining table or you could use it as a gift tag or glue it to a card as a decoration. Instructions for making this heart are given on page 42.

Valentine Baskets »

Woven heart baskets make the ideal containers for a Valentine's Day gift and create a fabulous first impression. For a lady the combination of red and white or red and gold are ideal, but for a gentleman you might prefer red and black. If it isn't the season for a Valentine gift, you could still make the baskets – what about a heart made in red and pink or two shades of blue to hold Mother's Day flowers? The red and gold woven heart shown here was made using the chequered template while the red and black one utilized the tile template (see page 118).

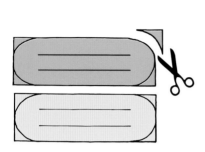

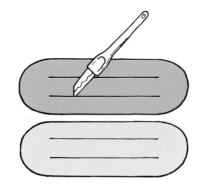

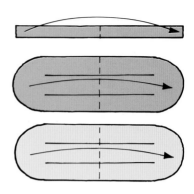

1 Trace and transfer your chosen template from page 118 onto the red and gold craft papers. Using the scissors, cut out the curved pieces but not the middle lines.

2 Using the craft knife, cutting mat and metal ruler, carefully cut along the solid middle lines of each curved piece, as shown, to make the strips.

3 Valley fold the strip of red paper and the curved pieces in half from side to side.

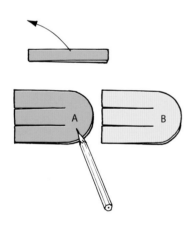

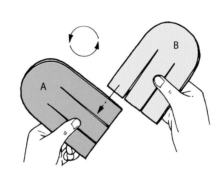

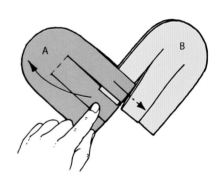

4 Using the pencil, lightly label one curved piece A and the other B. Place the handle aside for the moment.

5 Turn pieces A and B around into the position shown. A little patience is now required. Insert B's top strip between the layers of A's top strip.

6 Lift A's middle strip up. Insert A's top strip between the layers of B's middle strip, as shown.

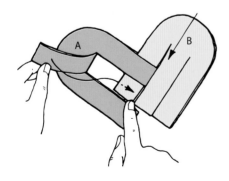

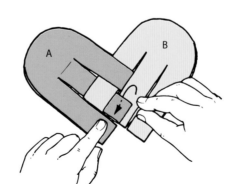

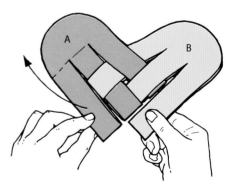

7 Slide piece B down a little. Insert A's middle strip between the layers of B's top strip, as shown.

8 Insert B's middle strip between the layers of A's middle strip.

9 Lift A's bottom strip up.

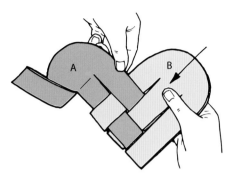

10 Again, slide piece B down a little.

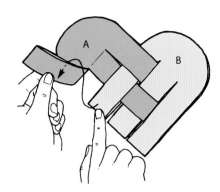

11 Bring A's bottom strip down. Now insert B's top strip between the layers of A's bottom strip.

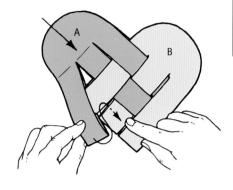

12 Slide piece A down a little. Insert A's bottom strip between the layers of B's middle strip.

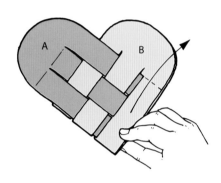

13 Lift B's bottom strip up.

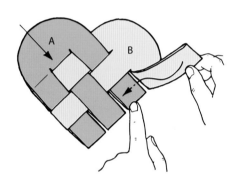

14 Slide piece A down as far as it will go. Insert B's bottom strip between the layers of A's top strip.

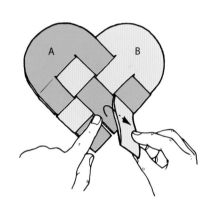

15 Insert A's middle strip between the layers of B's bottom strip.

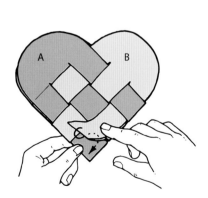

16 Finally, insert B's bottom strip between the layers of A's bottom strip. Erase the A and B pencil marks.

17 You now have a heart-shaped basket. Press the edges to open it. To finish, glue each end of the handle to the inside of the basket, as shown.

Flag Your Gift
Make the heart basket using the classic Danish flag design in its red and white colours or try red and silver to give it a little sparkle. This design uses the flag template on page 118.

Woven Heart Gift Basket

You will need

✓ 15cm (6in) square of red origami paper

✓ Basic tool kit

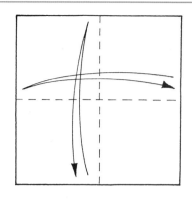

1 Fold and unfold the square of red origami paper in half from side to side and top to bottom, with the white side on top.

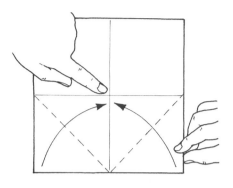

2 Valley fold the bottom corners in to the middle, as shown.

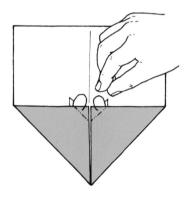

3 Mountain fold a little of each corner behind, as shown.

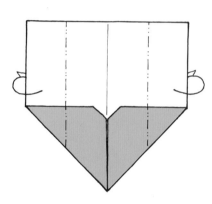

4 Mountain fold the sides behind to meet the middle fold-line.

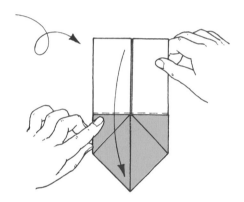

5 Turn the paper over. Valley fold in half from top to bottom.

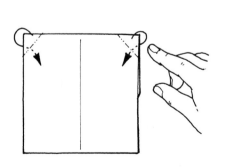

6 Inside reverse fold a little of each top corner…

7 down inside the model.

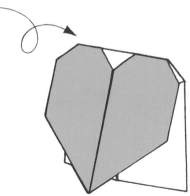

8 Turn the finished memo holder over.

Valentine Card

You will need

- ✓ Black two-panel card
- ✓ 7.5cm (3in) square of red origami paper
- ✓ 6.5cm (2⅝in) square of black craft paper
- ✓ 7cm (2¾in) square of red craft paper
- ✓ 7.5cm (3in) square of gold craft paper
- ✓ 30cm (12in) length of 1cm (⅜in) wide gold and black ribbon
- ✓ Red sticky-backed gem heart
- ✓ Basic tool kit

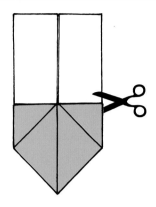

1 Begin by repeating steps 1 to 4 for the memo holder with the square of red origami paper. Turn the paper over and cut along its horizontal middle line. Place the white part aside as it is not required.

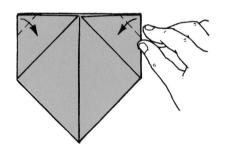

2 Valley fold a little of the red part's top corners over.

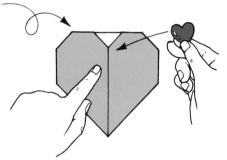

3 Turn the paper over to reveal a heart. Remove the backing from the red gem heart and attach it to the paper heart.

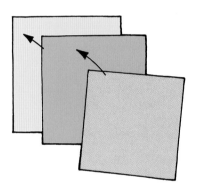

4 Layer the background squares, centrally, in the order gold, red and black. Glue them all together.

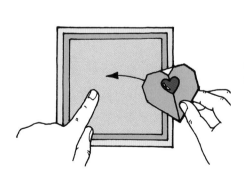

5 Apply glue to the back of the heart and mount it centrally on the stacked background squares.

6 Apply glue to the back of the squares and mount them on the front of the black two-panel card, slightly above the card's centre, as shown.

7 To finish, tie the length of gold and black ribbon into a bow and cut a V-shaped notch into each of the ends. Using double-sided tape, attach it to the card, slightly above the middle point of the gold square's top edge.

Summer Flower Picture

The perfect Mother's Day present, this delightful project shows how with a little imagination and some simple paper craft techniques you can capture the fleeting scent of a flower and the beauty of its petals. What is important here is your personal touch – the feelings that you inject into building up the components. These intangible qualities will breath life into the flowers and help you to send your message of affection.

You Will need

- ✓ 7.5cm (3in) square of pink origami paper for the vase
- ✓ Two 6cm (2⅜in) squares of green origami paper for the leaves
- ✓ Three 4cm (1⅝in) squares of pink origami paper for the flowers
- ✓ Three 4cm (1⅝in) squares of orange origami paper for the flowers
- ✓ 12 x 12.5cm (4¾ x 5in) piece of light brown craft card for the background
- ✓ Six 6cm (2⅜in) lengths of light green double-headed stamen strings
- ✓ 20cm (7⅞in) length of raffia for the bow
- ✓ Standard CD jewel case
- ✓ Small quantity of dried gypsophila
- ✓ Basic tool kit

This lovely floral arrangement is designed to fit on the front of a CD case. If you take digital photographs, why not put a selection of the latest family shots on a CD and send them off on Mother's Day in a CD case decorated in this way? Alternatively, use it to present an album of favourite music or a DVD. Even if you don't have a disc, you can still use this flower picture, mounting it on a greetings card or framing it to hang on the wall.

Build your bouquet using your favourite colours or papers. The mottled paper used for these pink flowers works wonderfully.

Mother's Day Gift »

Each element of this lovely card is made individually – the bow, vase, the two leaves and every flower. As you bring the flowers into bloom you'll find yourself arranging them in the vase with all the care and gentleness you would use for a fresh flower arrangement.

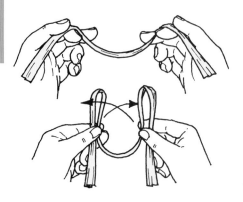

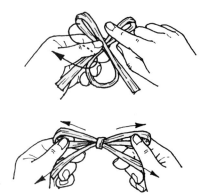

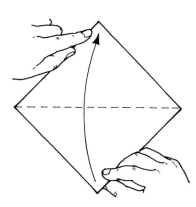

1 To make the bow, make two evenly spaced loops in the raffia, as shown, holding one in each hand. Cross the right loop over the left.

2 Take the right loop around to the back of the left, then forward through the hole created in the centre. To finish, pull the loops away from each other to tighten the centre. You may need to adjust the loops and tails to make the bow even before finally tightening the knot.

3 To make the vase, turn the square of pink origami paper around to look like a diamond, with the white side on top. Valley fold in half from bottom to top, making a diaper fold.

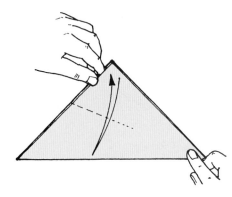

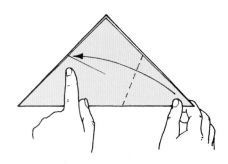

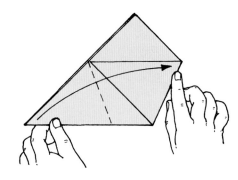

4 From the bottom right-hand point, valley fold the front flap of paper down to meet the bottom edge, but do not press the paper completely flat. Instead press it only a little as shown by the dashed lines. Return the flap to its original position.

5 Valley fold the bottom right-hand point over to meet the fold mark that was made in step 4.

6 Valley fold the bottom left-hand point over to meet the opposite side.

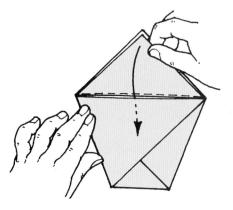

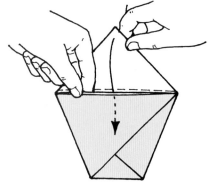

7 With a valley fold, insert the top point into the front triangular pocket.

8 Insert the remaining top point inside the model.

9 Push it down to finish the vase.

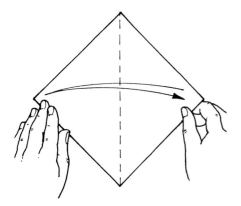

10 To make the leaves, turn one square of green origami paper around to look like a diamond, with the white side on top. Fold and unfold in half from right to left.

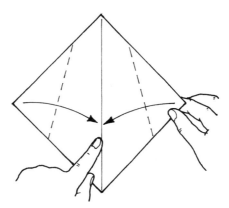

11 Valley fold the right- and left-hand side points in to meet the middle fold-line on a slant, as shown.

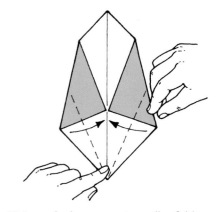

12 From the bottom point, valley fold the sloping edges in to meet the middle fold-line.

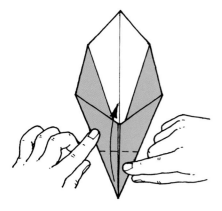

13 Valley fold the bottom point up, slightly beyond the point where the middle sloping edges meet, to make the stalk.

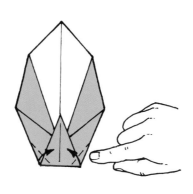

14 Valley fold a little of the stalk's bottom side points over on a slant.

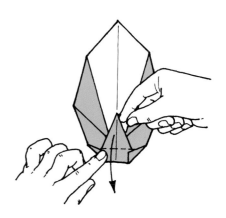

15 Valley fold the stalk down as far as it will go.

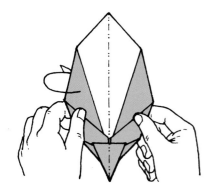

16 Mountain fold in half from left to right.

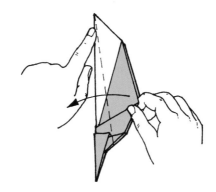

17 Valley fold the front flap of paper over to the left on a slant, as shown, to finish one leaf.

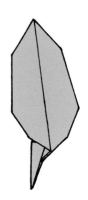

18 Repeat steps 10 to 17 with the remaining square of green origami paper.

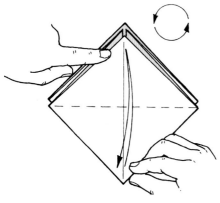

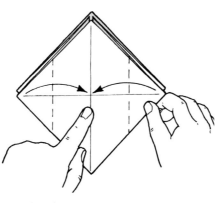

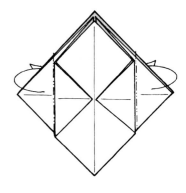

19 To make the flowers, repeat steps 1 to 7 for the yellow flower card on pages 22–23 with one flower square of origami paper, but with the coloured side on top in step 1. Turn the preliminary fold around, so that the open layers are pointing away from you. Fold and unfold in half from bottom to top.

20 Valley fold the top side points in to the middle.

21 Mountain fold the bottom side points in to the middle.

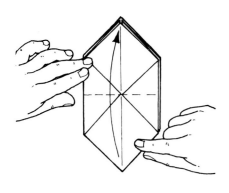

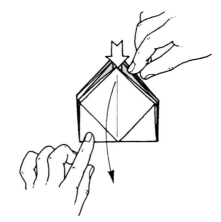

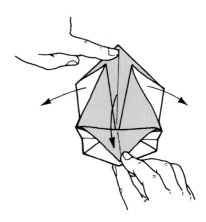

22 Valley fold the bottom point up to meet the top points.

23 Pinch the bottom point and topmost point together. Pull them down, so that the inside points rise up.

24 Flatten the folded edge of each point down to each side to make petals.

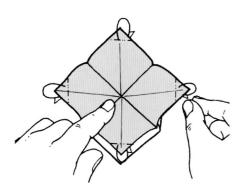

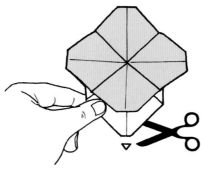

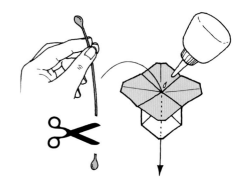

25 Mountain fold a little of the petals' tips behind. Press the paper flat.

26 Snip off the bottom point, making a tiny hole.

27 Cut off one of the heads from a light green stamen string. Apply a little glue around the flower's middle. Insert the stamen string's bottom end into the flower and out through the hole.

28 Pull the stamen string down until its head comes to rest in the glued area to finish one flower. Repeat steps 19 to 28 with the remaining five flower squares of origami paper and stamen strings.

29 To assemble the picture, turn the piece of light brown craft card sideways on. Apply glue to the back of the vase and mount it on the craft card near the middle of the bottom edge.

30 Insert the leaves into the vase from each side. Glue them into place.

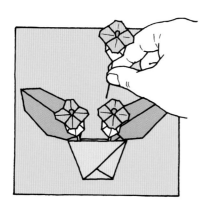

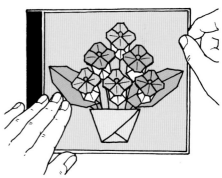

31 Arrange the flowers around the vase so that they are closely packed together. When you are satisfied with the arrangement, glue the flowers onto the craft card.

32 Apply a strip of double-sided tape to each side of the jewel case's front cover.

33 Remove the backing from the strips of double-sided tape and carefully mount the back of the flower arrangement onto them, as shown.

34 To finish, attach the bow on the vase with a small piece of double-sided tape and glue little sprays of dried gypsophila into the arrangement.

Flower Arranging »
All the elements of this picture are created individually, giving you the chance to do a little flower arranging of your own. You can also use any colour combination for the flowers, such as the popular mix of blue and yellow used here.

Stylish Gift Bags

When you have selected the best possible present, you'll want the wrapping to be as elegant as the gift and give an exciting first impression. These unusual mannequin-style bags will do the trick and are sure to cause a stir. There is only one drawback: your recipients may like the outside packaging so much, they may never unwrap the presents!

You will need

For the blouse

- ✓ 50 x 70cm (19¾ x 27½in) sheet of handmade gift wrap
- ✓ 60cm (23⅝in) length of 3cm (1¼in) wide wine-coloured ribbon
- ✓ Basic tool kit

For the tuxedo

- ✓ 50 x 70cm (19¾ x 27½in) sheet of white gift wrap
- ✓ 42 x 70cm (16½ x 27½in) sheet of black gift wrap
- ✓ 7.5 x 15cm (3 x 6in) rectangle of tartan gift wrap for the bow tie
- ✓ Three gold sticky-backed gems
- ✓ Basic tool kit

These creative gift bags are very easy to make and once you have learned the basic technique you'll probably come up with your own variations. For the lady's bag you'll only need one sheet of gift wrap and some ribbon for the tie, while you'll need two sheets of gift wrap for the tuxedo, one white and one black, plus a brighter gift wrap for the bow tie and some stick-on gems for buttons. Just as on the real clothing, it's the extras, such as the tie and buttons, that add character, so choose these carefully to look chic, cheerful or outrageous, depending on your own sense of style. The finished bags are 40cm (15¾in) high.

« Fashion Flair

The jaunty bow tie and shiny gem buttons complete the tuxedo and give it a fashionable look. The tie is made independently in just eight steps, and makes a nice finishing touch for other items. It is used on the bear on page 108, for example.

Ladies and Gentlemen »

Emulating the clothing for a very fine event, these bags hint that they contain something superior or the ultimate in luxury. What you decide to put in them is up to you, but the bags will set the tone.

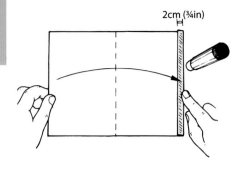

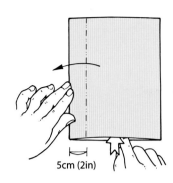

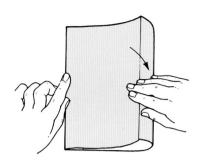

1 Place the gift wrap sideways on, with the plain side on top. Valley fold the right-hand side over, making a 2cm (¾in) wide band of paper. Apply glue along the band. Valley fold the paper in half from left to right.

2 Press firmly to make a tube. Slide 5cm (2in) of the tube's top layer over to the left, making…

3 the right-hand side rise up. Press the tube down neatly into its new position.

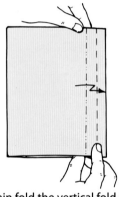

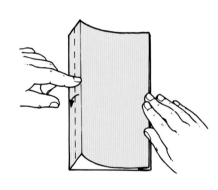

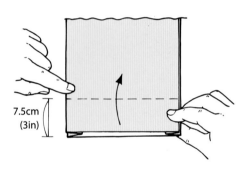

4 Mountain fold the vertical fold-line over to meet the right-hand side to pleat the paper, making the left-hand side rise up, as shown in step 5.

5 Fold the vertical 'folded' edge down to meet the left-hand side, so pleating the paper once again.

6 Treating all the bottom layers of paper as if they were one, valley fold them up along a horizontal line that is 7.5cm (3in) away from the bottom edge to make a flap of paper.

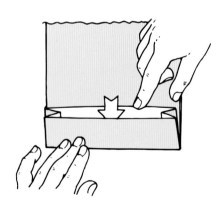

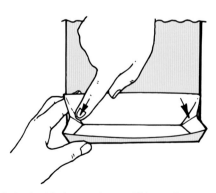

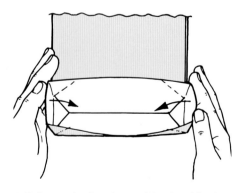

7 Stand the flap upright. Open it out, so that…

8 the inside layers rise up. Flatten the folded edge of each layer to form triangles and make an open box-like shape.

9 Collapse the box by pushing its sides in, so that they lie flat against the triangles and make tapered flaps.

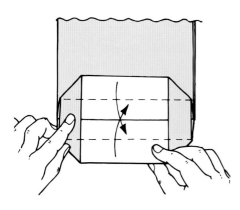

10 Valley fold the bottom tapered flap over on a line between the adjacent side points. Repeat with the top tapered flap.

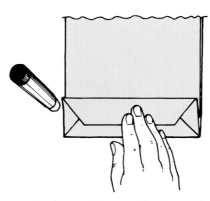

11 Glue the top flap onto the bottom flap. Press firmly. You now have a flat gift bag.

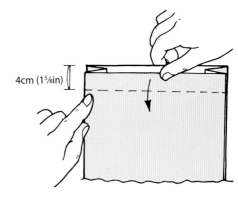

4cm (1⅝in)

12 Treating all the top layers of paper as if they were one, valley fold them down along a horizontal line that is 4cm (1⅝in) away from the top edge to make the blouse's collar.

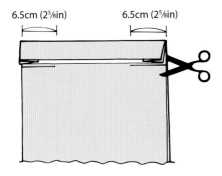

6.5cm (2⅝in)   6.5cm (2⅝in)

13 From each side of the collar, along its bottom edge, make two 6.5cm (2⅝in) horizontal cuts, as shown.

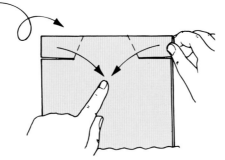

14 Turn the gift bag over. Valley fold each end of the collar over on a slant.

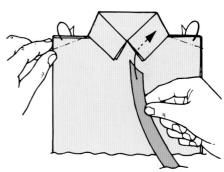

15 Mountain fold the bag's top corners behind on a slant. Insert the length of ribbon between the collar's layers, so that it protrudes equally on each side.

16 To finish, tie the ends of the ribbon into a bow. The actual tying of the bow will hold the gift bag together. To insert your present, untie the bow and unfold the gift bag back to step 12. Place your present inside. Close the bag up and redo steps 12 to 16.

Adding Strength »
The gift bags can be made any size, but the larger the bag the thicker the paper should be. If a heavy gift is to be placed inside, it is advisable to glue a piece of card inside the base of the bag. To strengthen the top of the bag, add an extra strip of paper under the collar.

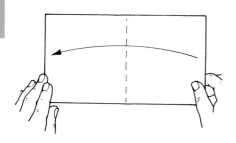

1 To make the bow tie, place the tartan gift wrap sideways on, with the white side on top. Valley fold in half from right to left.

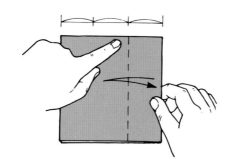

2 Valley fold the right-hand side over to a point one-third of the way to the left. Press flat and unfold.

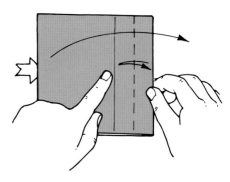

3 Valley fold the right-hand side over to meet the fold-line made in step 2. Press flat and unfold. Open out the paper from left to right.

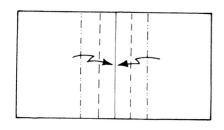

4 Along the fold-lines made in steps 2 and 3, pleat the paper on each side of the middle fold-line, with the white side on top, as shown.

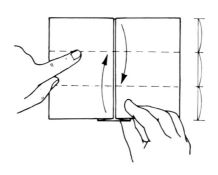

5 Divide the paper into three across its width by first valley folding the bottom edge up and then the top edge down.

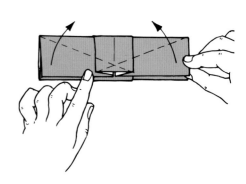

6 Valley fold the front layer's bottom corners up on a slant.

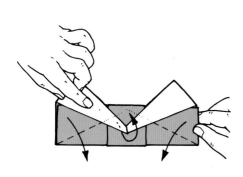

7 Separate the back layer of paper from the front layer, so that it lies on top. Valley fold its top corners down on a slant.

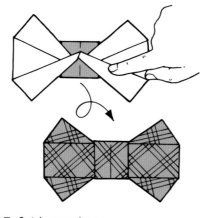

8 To finish, turn the paper over.

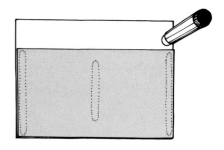

9 To make the bag, turn both sheets of gift wrap sideways on. Place the black gift wrap on top of the white gift wrap, aligning their bottom edges and sides. Glue them both together as shown by the x-ray lines. Press firmly.

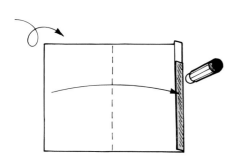

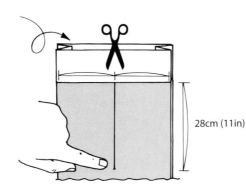

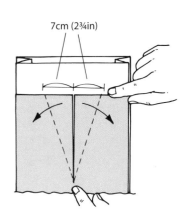

10 Carefully turn the gift wraps over from side to side. Treating both layers of gift wrap as if they were one, repeat steps 1 to 11 for the blouse gift bag.

11 Turn the bag over. Using the scissors, cut a 28cm (11in) long slit, down the black layer's vertical middle line, as shown.

12 From a point 7cm (2¾in) on each side of the start of the slit, valley fold the middle corners out on a line that connects with the end of the slit.

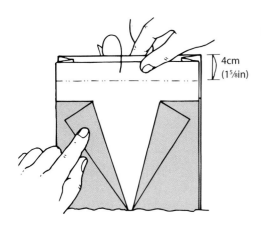

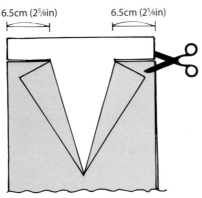

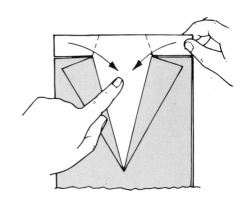

13 Treating all the top layers of paper as if they were one, mountain fold them behind along a horizontal line that is 4cm (1⅝in) away from the top edge, making the tuxedo's collar.

14 From each side of the collar, along its bottom edge, make two 6.5cm (2⅝in) horizontal cuts, as shown.

15 Valley fold each end of the collar over on a slant.

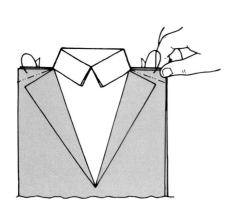

16 Mountain fold the bag's top corners behind on a slant. To insert your present, unfold the gift bag back to step 13. Place your present inside. Close the bag up and redo steps 13 to 16.

17 Apply glue to the back of the bow tie and mount it on the gift bag slightly over the collar. To finish, remove the backing from the gold gems and attach them in a row down the bag's middle line, as shown.

Christmas Greetings

The concept of sending a Christmas card is relatively new – the first ones were printed in 1846, and were the idea of Henry Cole, who was the first director of the Victoria and Albert Museum in London. At first the idea wasn't successful, but these days most people send and receive many cards, the majority of which end up in the bin after the holidays. These cards will be different. They are items to treasure because they were made by you.

You will need

For the stocking card

✓ Red three-panel window card

✓ 8cm (3⅛in) square of red origami paper

✓ 9cm (3½in) square of green and silver-star patterned paper for the background

✓ 15cm (6in) length of 1cm (⅜in) wide red tartan ribbon

✓ Crystal glitter glue

✓ One small red and one small white pompom

✓ Four three-dimensional craft holly leaves

✓ Four small shiny silver stars

✓ Basic tool kit

These colourful Christmas cards are all based on a three-panel window card that you can easily make yourself (see page 14). Each one features a traditional motif – a stocking, Santa or candle – made out of folded paper and mounted on a contrasting background paper behind the window. Ribbons and craft embellishments complete the look.

The image of the stocking reminds us of the gifts that will be given and received at Christmas. Handmade items, such as this card, are always so much nicer to receive than those that have been purchased.

Christmas Specials »

Combining traditional colours and motifs with modern origami methods, these cards are a joy to make and a pleasure to receive. Your cards will literally stand out beside ordinary shop-bought Christmas cards because of their three-dimensional origami motifs. The gold and silver trimmings will glitter in the light for a lavish, festive note.

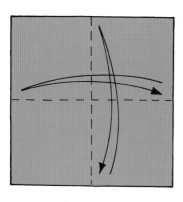

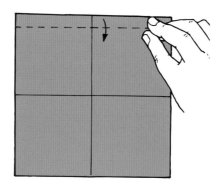

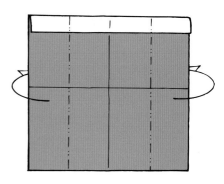

1 To make the stocking, fold and unfold the square of red origami paper in half from side to side and top to bottom, with the coloured side on top.

2 Valley fold down a little of the top edge, making a band of white paper.

3 Mountain fold the sides behind to meet the middle fold-line.

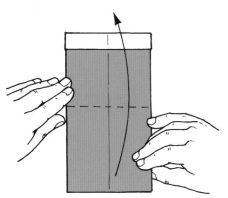

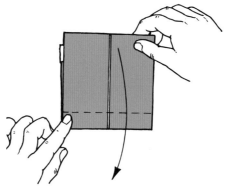

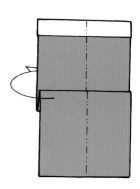

4 Valley fold the bottom edge up along the existing horizontal fold-line.

5 Valley fold the front flap of paper down so that it makes a small pleat.

6 Mountain fold in half from left to right.

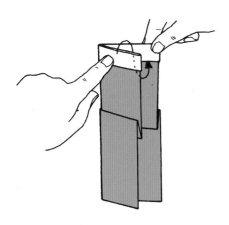

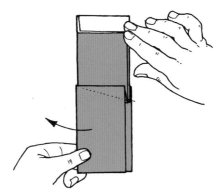

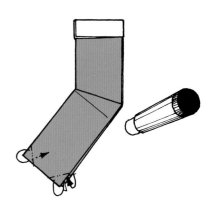

7 Insert one band of paper inside the other, as shown.

8 Pull the bottom section of paper up as far as the hidden pleat will allow to make the stocking's toe.

9 Inside reverse fold the toe's top corner down and mountain fold its bottom corners up inside the model. Finally, glue the stocking's inside layers together.

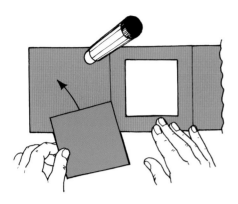

10 To prepare the card, open out the red three-panel window card completely. Apply glue to the back of the green background square and mount it centrally on the card's left-hand panel.

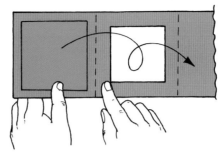

11 Valley fold the panels over and over from left to right.

12 Using the hole punch, create a hole in the card's top left-hand corner. Loop the length of red tartan ribbon in half and pass the looped end through the hole.

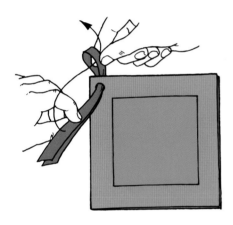

13 Thread the other ends of the ribbon through the loop. Pull tight to make a loop knot.

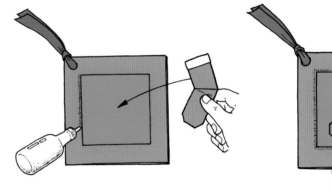

14 To assemble the card, apply glue to the back of the stocking and mount it on the background square. Apply a line of glitter glue around the window.

15 Glue the red and white pompoms onto the stocking's upper right-hand corner.

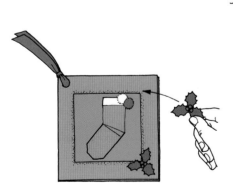

16 Glue a craft holly leaf to each corner of the window, as shown.

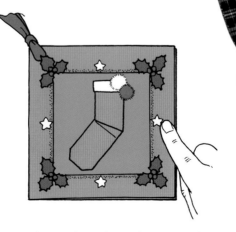

17 To finish, glue a shiny silver star to the middle of the window's edges.

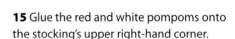

59

You will need

For the Santa card

✓ Dark red three-panel window card

✓ 6cm (2⅜in) square of red origami paper for the body

✓ 3cm (1³⁄₁₆in) square of red origami paper for the face

✓ 9cm (3½in) square of green and gold speckled paper for the background

✓ 15cm (6in) length of 0.7cm (⁵⁄₁₆in) wide burgundy and gold striped ribbon

✓ Crystal glitter glue

✓ Two small white pompoms

✓ Two three-dimensional craft poinsettias

✓ Medium and small shiny gold stars

✓ Basic tool kit

Santa Card

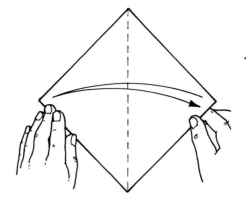

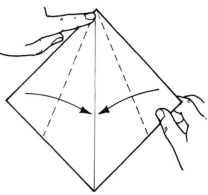

1 To make the Santa body, turn the body square of red origami paper around to look like a diamond, with the white side on top. Fold and unfold in half from right to left.

2 From the top point, valley fold the sloping edges in to meet the middle fold-line. Press them flat, making a kite base.

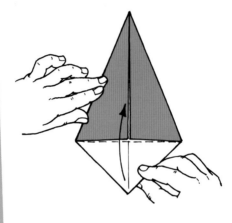

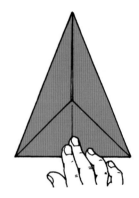

3 Valley fold the white triangle up along the base of the coloured triangle.

4 Press the paper flat.

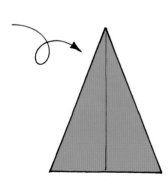

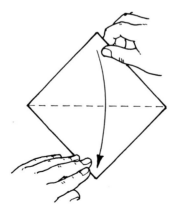

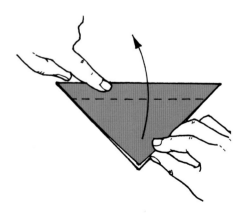

5 Finally, turn the paper over.

6 To make the face, turn the face square of red origami paper around to look like a diamond, with the white side on top. Valley fold in half from top to bottom, making a diaper fold.

7 Valley fold the front flap of paper up, making a small pleat.

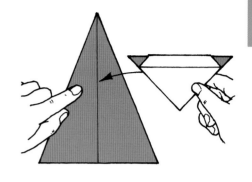

8 Mountain fold the top point behind along the line of the adjacent horizontal edge, making the hat's brim.

9 Press the paper flat.

10 To assemble the Santa, place the face on the body, as shown.

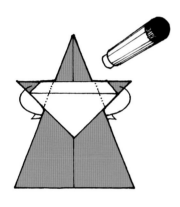

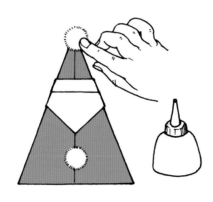

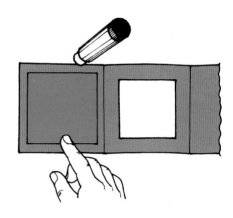

11 Mountain fold the face's side points behind along the line of the body's sloping edges. Glue them down.

12 Decorate Santa by gluing one small white pompom on the hat's top point and the remaining one on the middle of his body, as shown.

13 To prepare the card, repeat steps 10 and 11 for the stocking on page 59 with the dark red three-panel window card and green background square.

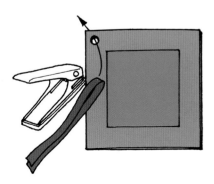

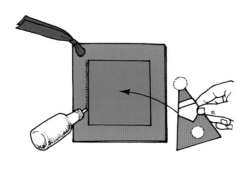

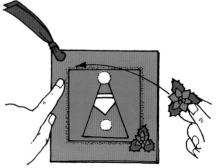

14 Repeat steps 12 and 13 for the stocking with the length of burgundy and gold striped ribbon.

15 To assemble the card, apply glue to the back of the Santa and mount him on the background square. Apply a line of glitter glue around the window.

16 Glue a craft poinsettia to the window's lower right- and upper left-hand corners. To finish, glue the shiny gold stars around the window.

Candlestick Card

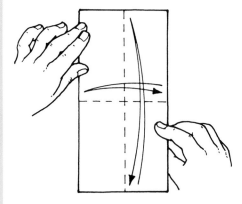

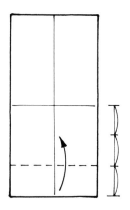

You will need

For the candlestick card

- ✓ Green three-panel window card
- ✓ 6 x 12cm (2⅜ x 4¾in) piece of gold origami paper
- ✓ 9cm (3½in) square of red and silver star patterned paper for the background
- ✓ 15cm (6in) length of 0.7cm (⁵⁄₁₆in) wide green checked ribbon
- ✓ Crystal glitter glue
- ✓ Three-dimensional craft poinsettia
- ✓ Two craft snowflakes (one white and one green)
- ✓ Two adhesive foam pads
- ✓ Small shiny coloured stars
- ✓ Basic tool kit

1 To make the candlestick, place the piece of gold origami paper lengthways on, with the white side on top. Fold and unfold in half from side to side and top to bottom.

2 Valley fold the bottom edge up to a point one-third of the way to the middle, making a flap.

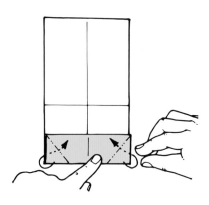

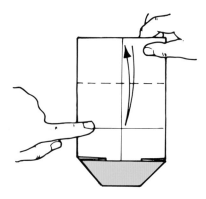

3 Valley fold the bottom corners up to meet the flap's top edge. Press flat and unfold. Using the fold-lines just made as a guide, inside reverse fold the bottom corners up inside the flap.

4 Valley fold the top edge down to meet the horizontal fold-line, as shown. Press flat and unfold.

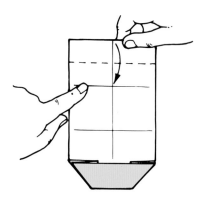

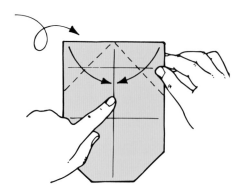

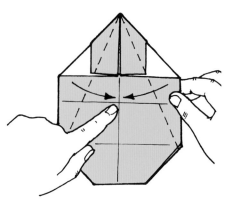

5 Valley fold the top edge down to meet the fold-line made in step 4.

6 Turn the paper over. Valley fold the top corners down to meet the middle vertical fold-line.

7 From the top point, valley fold the sloping edges in to meet the middle vertical fold-line.

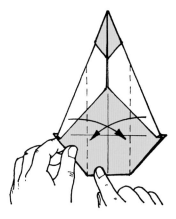

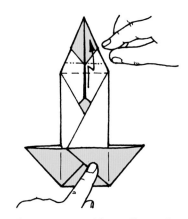

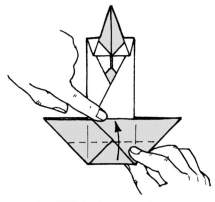

8 Valley fold the left-hand sloping edges over, as shown. Repeat with the right-hand sloping edges so that they lie on top.

9 Pleat the top point with a valley and mountain fold, as shown, making the candle's flame.

10 Valley fold the bottom edge up so that it meets the adjacent horizontal edge.

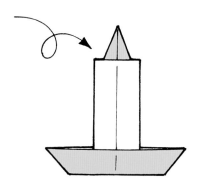

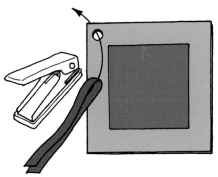

11 Turn the paper over.

12 To prepare the card, repeat steps 10 and 11 for the stocking on page 59 with the green three-panel window card and red background square.

13 Repeat steps 12 and 13 for the stocking with the length of green checked ribbon.

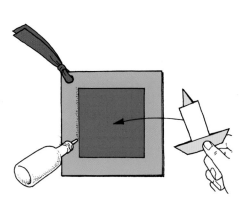

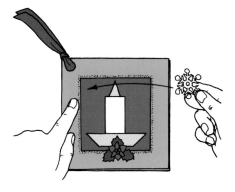

14 To assemble the card, apply glue to the back of the candlestick and mount it on the background square. Apply a line of glitter glue around the window.

15 Glue the craft poinsettia to the middle of the window's bottom edge.

16 Attach the craft snowflakes (green snowflake slightly over the white one) to the background square's upper left-hand corner with adhesive foam pads. To finish, glue the shiny stars to the card's upper right- and lower left-hand corners.

Tasselled Photo Wallet

Anyone who has children or grandchildren likes to be able to carry one or two choice photographs about with them, and this exquisite photo wallet is ideal for that purpose. It's also a lovely means of presenting a photograph of any important event to a family member or friend, be it of a birth, wedding, reunion or memorable outing. It is a gift that is guaranteed to bring pleasure throughout the year. The accompanying wallet is practical and smart. Use it for storing loyalty cards, vouchers, business cards or stamps.

You will need

For the photo wallet

✓ 28cm (11in) square of swirled patterned vellum paper

✓ 28cm (11in) square of blue handmade paper

✓ 20cm (8in) length of looped tasselled cord – if unavailable, use a 40cm (16in) length of single cord that is tasselled at both ends

✓ Bead with a 0.3cm ($\frac{1}{8}$in) diameter hole

✓ Photograph no larger than 10 x 15cm (4 x 6in)

✓ Basic tool kit

For the voucher wallet

✓ 35cm (13¾in) square of yellow handmade paper for the pocket

✓ 35 x 70cm (13¾ x 27½in) piece of white pearlescent paper for the flap

This elegant photo wallet combines vellum and handmade papers to excellent effect, although you could experiment with other papers, if desired. The papers are layered in a staggered formation so that the handmade paper forms an attractive border on the flap. The vellum makes the ideal top paper because its translucency allows the colour of the handmade paper to show through. The wallet is constructed in a similar way to an envelope, and the photograph hidden inside, so the recipient won't know what's in store until they remove the tasselled tie and lift the flaps.

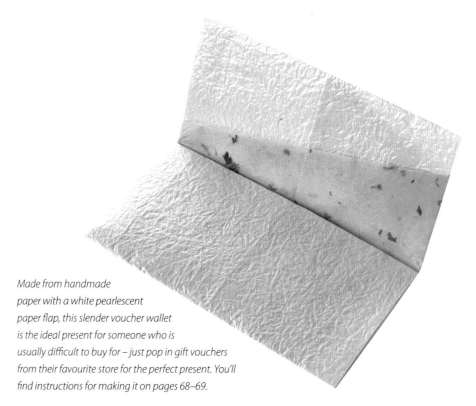

Made from handmade paper with a white pearlescent paper flap, this slender voucher wallet is the ideal present for someone who is usually difficult to buy for – just pop in gift vouchers from their favourite store for the perfect present. You'll find instructions for making it on pages 68–69.

Photograph Wallet »

Made in a lovely combination of vellum and handmade papers, this elegant photo wallet would be ideal for storing or presenting a wedding photograph or other precious image. You might wish to choose papers that tie in with the enclosed photograph in some way.

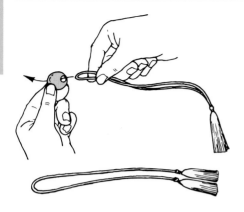

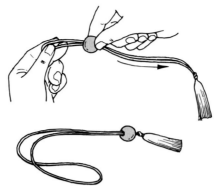

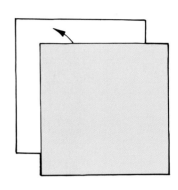

1 Prepare the cord. If you are using a length of cord that is tasselled at both ends, loop it in half. Thread the looped end of your cord through the bead.

2 Pull the bead along the cord to meet the tasselled end(s).

3 To make the photo wallet, place the square of blue handmade paper on top of the square of vellum, with the vellum's plain side facing up.

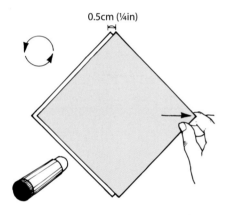

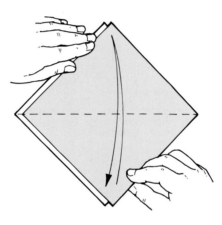

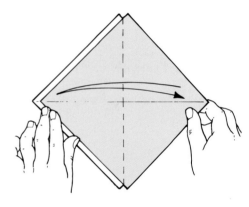

4 Turn the squares around to look like a diamond. Pull the blue square 0.5cm (¼in) to the right to reveal the vellum's left-hand sloping edges. Glue the squares together at their middle points.

5 From now onwards treat both layers of paper as if they were one. Fold and unfold in half from bottom to top.

6 Fold and unfold in half from right to left.

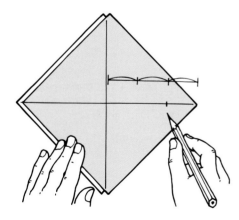

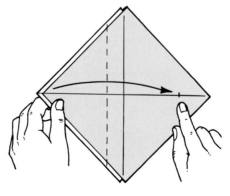

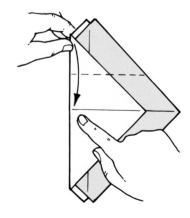

7 Using the pencil and ruler, mark and measure a point that is one third of the way to the middle from the right-hand point, as shown.

8 Valley fold the left-hand point over to meet the pencil mark made in step 7.

9 Valley fold the top left-hand side point down to meet the middle fold-line.

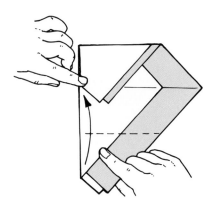

10 Valley fold the bottom left-hand side point up to meet the middle fold-line.

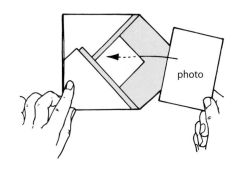

11 Turn your photograph lengthways on and insert it deep into the layers of paper.

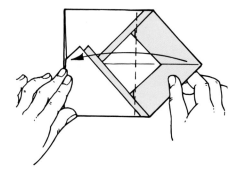

12 Valley fold the right-hand point over to meet the middle of the left-hand side, making a flap.

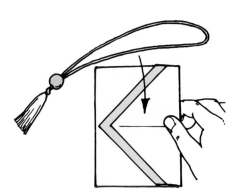

13 Slip the looped cord over the wallet.

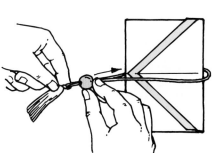

14 Push the bead across the cord, towards the wallet, fastening the flap down.

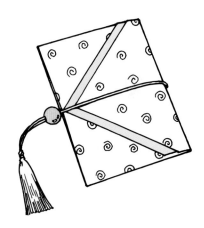

15 The bead will neatly hold the photo wallet closed.

Easy Open »
To open the photo wallet, all you have to do is slide the bead back towards the tassels, slip the cord off and then unwrap the paper.

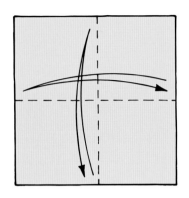

1 To make the pocket, fold and unfold the square of yellow handmade paper in half from side to side and top to bottom, with the plain side on top.

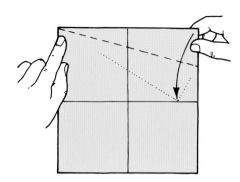

2 From the top left-hand corner, valley fold the top right-hand corner down to meet the middle fold-line.

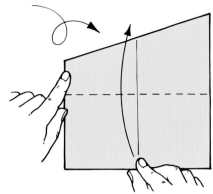

3 Turn the paper over from side to side. Valley fold in half from bottom to top.

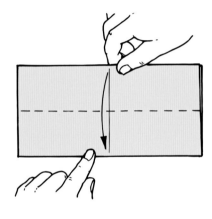

4 Valley fold the front flap of paper in half from top to bottom.

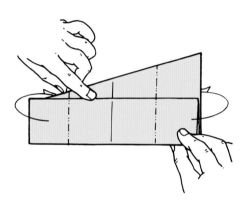

5 Mountain fold the sides behind to meet the middle fold-line.

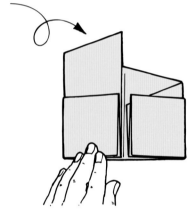

6 Turn the paper over from side to side. This finishes the pocket.

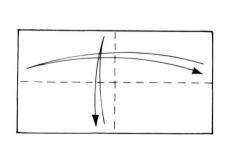

7 To make the flap, place the piece of white pearlescent paper sideways on, with the plain side on top. Fold and unfold in half from side to side and top to bottom.

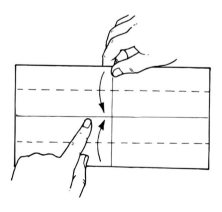

8 Valley fold the top and bottom edges in to meet the middle. This finishes the flap.

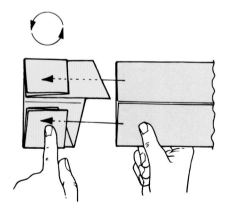

9 To assemble the wallet, turn the pocket sideways on. Insert the flap deep into the pocket, as shown.

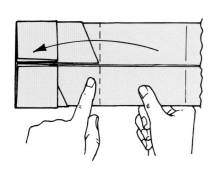

10 Using the pocket's sloping edge as a guide to the position of the fold-line, valley fold the flap over to the left.

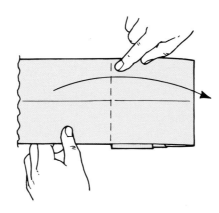

11 Using the underneath left-hand side as a guide to the position of the fold-line, valley fold the flap over to the right, pleating the paper.

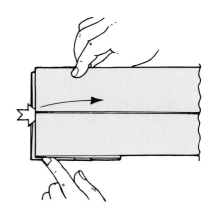

12 Lift up the pleat.

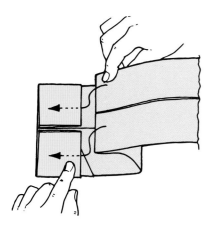

13 Insert the pleat underneath the top left-hand layers of paper.

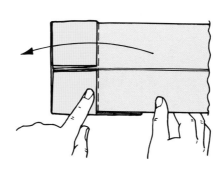

14 Using the vertical folded edges as a guide to the position of the fold-line, valley fold the flap over to the left.

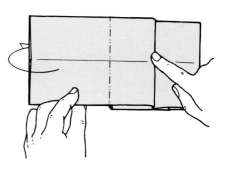

15 Using the underneath left-hand side as a guide to the position of the fold-line, mountain fold the flap behind.

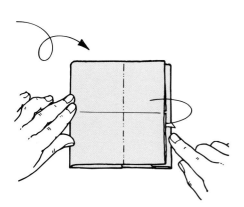

16 Turn the paper over. With a mountain fold, inset the end of the flap deep …

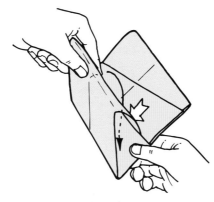

17 into the model, as shown.

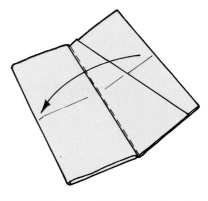

18 To finish, valley fold the right-hand pocketed section across to the left.

Two-colour Gift Box

Unit origami is a new way of folding paper by joining parts to form objects – in this case a square box with lid. Folding and assembling the units is a very simple process, and by working in sections you are given the opportunity to introduce different papers for decorative effect. Folded into this box is a delightful, intricate pattern that only origami can yield.

You will need

For the small box

✓ Two 12cm (4¾in) squares of blue and marble gift wrap and two 12cm (4¾in) squares of gold gift wrap for the base

✓ Two 12cm (4¾in) squares of blue and marble gift wrap and two 12cm (4¾in) squares of gold gift wrap for the lid

For the medium box

✓ Two 15cm (6in) squares of burgundy gift wrap and two 15cm (6in) squares of dark floral gift wrap for the base

✓ Two 15cm (6in) squares of burgundy gift wrap and two 15cm (6in) squares of dark floral gift wrap for the lid

For the large box

✓ Two 18cm (7⅛in) squares of black reptile skin gift wrap (plain on reverse) and two 18cm (7⅛in) squares of gold gift wrap for the base

✓ Two 18cm (7⅛in) squares of black reptile skin gift wrap (plain on reverse) and two 18cm (7⅛in) squares of gold gift wrap for the lid

This box is made in units – four for the base and four for the lid – that slot together to create the final shape. By using two colours of paper and slotting the different ones together alternately you can create an attractive and striking patchwork effect, as we did here. Use colours that contrast for a bold effect, or similar ones such as black and burgundy or pink and red for a subtle look. If you choose carefully, you could even use a different paper for each unit, which would produce a really intriguing effect.

There are three sizes of box to choose from, all made in the same way. The small box is 6 x 6 x 3cm (2⅜ x 2⅜ x 1³⁄₁₆in), the medium box is 7.5 x 7.5 x 3.75cm (3 x 3 x 1½in) and the large box is 9 x 9 x 4.5cm (3½ x 3½ x 1¾in).

« Finishing Touch
Subtly coordinating papers give this box an expensively elegant look. A ribbon tie makes a lovely finishing touch or you could use stickers if you prefer.

Great Gifts »
Attractive boxes, like the ones shown here, can make even the most inexpensive gift look special, and no doubt the recipient will want to keep the box afterwards as a storage container. We have used one patterned paper and one plain paper for each box because this creates an elegant effect. The metallic paper works especially well to give added glamour.

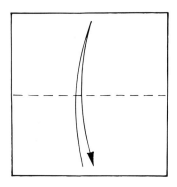

1 To make the base, fold and unfold one base square of gift wrap in half from bottom to top, with the plain side on top.

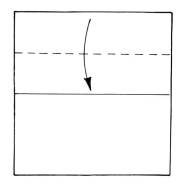

2 Valley fold the top edge down to meet the middle fold-line.

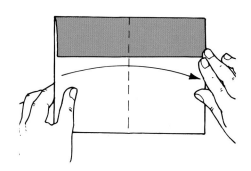

3 Valley fold in half from left to right.

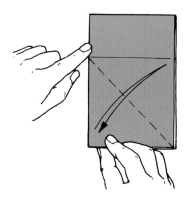

4 Valley fold the bottom left-hand corner up to meet the right-hand side. Press flat and unfold.

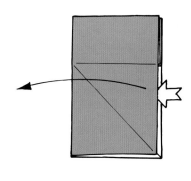

5 Open out the paper from right to left.

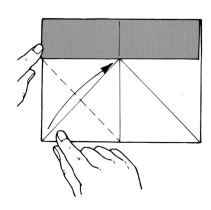

6 Valley fold the bottom left-hand corner up to meet the horizontal edge.

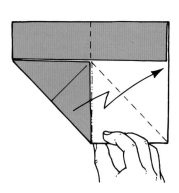

7 Put in the valley and mountain folds, as shown, making the left-hand section of paper stand upright.

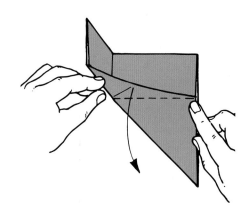

8 Valley fold the upright section down towards you along the horizontal fold-line.

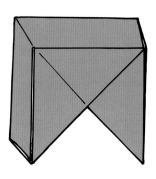

9 The two sides stand upright. This completes one base unit. Repeat steps 1 to 9 with the remaining three base squares.

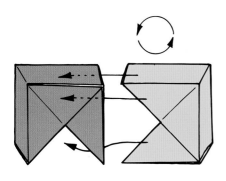

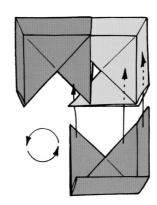

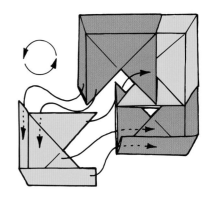

10 To assemble the base, insert one unit into the side and bottom pockets of another, tucking it between the pockets' front and back layers. Alternate the units and work clockwise.

11 Repeat step 10 with another unit.

12 Carefully insert the last unit into place, making sure it is positioned exactly as shown above.

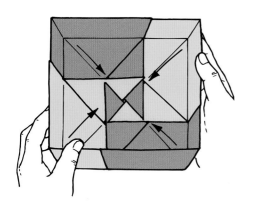

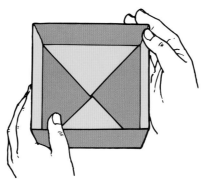

13 Gently push the units together…

14 until they form a square. This finishes the base.

Box Lid

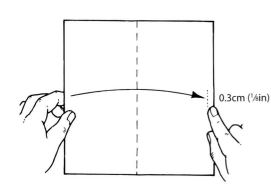

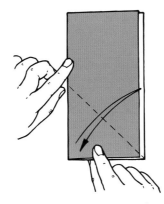

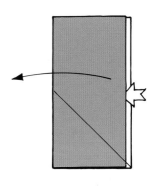

0.3cm (⅛in)

1 To make the lid, place one lid square on your working surface, plain side up. Valley fold the left-hand side over to a point that is 0.3cm (⅛in) from the right-hand side.

2 Valley fold the bottom left-hand corner up to meet the right-hand side. Press flat and unfold.

3 Open out the paper from right to left.

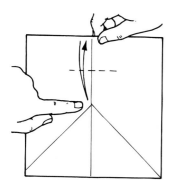

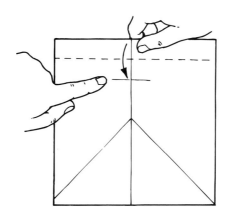

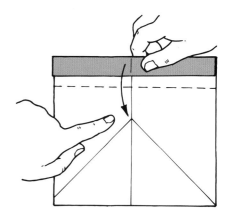

4 Valley fold the top edge down to meet the top of the diagonal fold-lines. Do not press the paper flat, but only mark it as shown by the dashed lines. Return the top edge to its original position.

5 Valley fold the top edge down to meet the fold mark made in step 4.

6 Valley fold the top edge down to meet the top of the diagonal fold-lines.

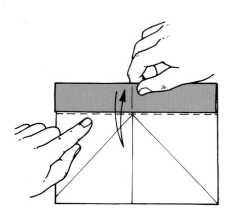

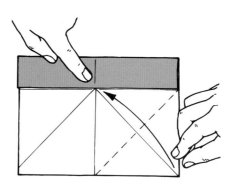

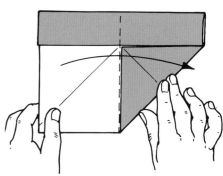

7 Valley fold the top edge down on a horizontal line that runs across the top of the diagonal fold-lines, as shown. Press flat and unfold.

8 Valley fold the bottom right-hand corner up to meet the horizontal edge.

9 Valley fold in half from left to right.

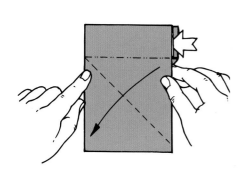

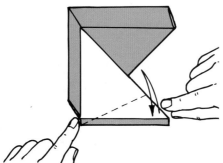

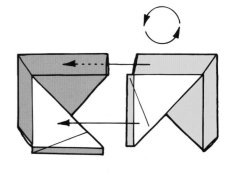

10 On the front flap of paper, put in the valley and mountain folds, as shown, making the two sides stand upright.

11 Valley fold the bottom edge up so that it lies along the diagonal line that runs from top right to bottom left, making a flap of paper. Press flat and unfold. This completes one lid unit. Repeat steps 1 to 11 with the remaining three lid squares.

12 To assemble the lid, insert one unit into the side pocket of another, at the same time arranging its creased flap (see step 11) to lie on top of the other unit's flap, as shown. Alternate the units and work clockwise.

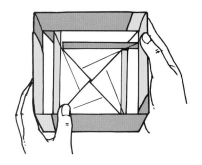

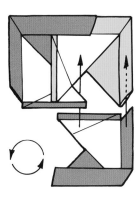

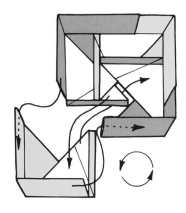

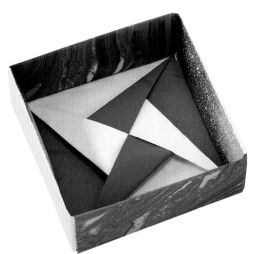

13 Repeat step 12 with another unit.

14 Carefully insert the last unit into place, making sure it is positioned exactly as shown above.

15 Gently push the units together, until they form a square.

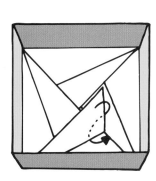

16 Working anti-clockwise, valley fold the flaps along their existing fold-lines to lie over each other, as shown in step 17.

17 Tuck the last flap underneath the adjacent one, locking the units together. This completes the lid. To finish, turn the lid over and slip it over the base.

Box Lid »
The box lid is constructed in a different way to the base to ensure that it will be slightly wider to sit snugly over the top. The pattern of folds on the inside of the lid also creates added decorative detail (see above right).

Iris Folded Cards

Iris folding is a simple yet lovely technique that originated in the Netherlands. Strips of paper are folded in half, trimmed to size and arranged in a circular pattern, producing a design rather like the inside of a camera lens (which is how iris folding got its name). To use this technique for cards, the folded paper can be placed behind an aperture and glued to a two-panel card. Additional card shapes, stickers and any other embellishments can be added to complete the look.

You will need

For the pumpkin card

✓ Black two-panel card

✓ 9 x 11cm (3½ x 4¼in) rectangle of orange card for the pumpkin aperture

✓ 12 x 15cm (4¾ x 6in) rectangle of orange card for the pumpkin mat

✓ 10 x 12cm (4 x 4¾in) rectangle of black card for the pumpkin shadow

✓ Four 2 x 40cm (¾ x 15¾in) rectangles of giftwrap or patterned paper for the iris folds: one each in green, red, yellow and orange

✓ 2cm (¾in) square of dark purple paper

✓ Star sticker for the centre

✓ Halloween stickers such as bats, moons, witches and pumpkins

✓ Deckle-edged scissors

✓ Adhesive foam pads

✓ Basic tool kit

The four cards on these pages were inspired by the colours and themes of autumn and highlight one of the season's most popular events – Halloween. There's a glorious pumpkin card to make in the warm colours of harvest, and a spooky bat in striking black and silver. For a more general autumn greeting try the elegant owl or autumn leaf card (page 79), which would also look lovely framed as pictures. These are made in the same way as the pumpkin card (explained overleaf) but utilizing different designs.

« Night Owl

This owl card utilizes metallic paper for a luxurious note, and uses the owl template and folding pattern on page 114. The delicate skeleton leaves and gold peel-offs are the ideal finishing touch.

Halloween Favourites »
You'll have lots of fun making these spooky Halloween cards to send to family and friends. Follow the instructions overleaf for the pumpkin, then make the bat in the same way, using the bat template and folding pattern on page 114. The bat card has a clever background of silver card cut to fit the left half of the card front, then trimmed with deckle-edged scissors. The silver band is cut using the same scissors.

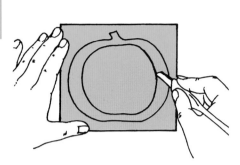

1 To prepare, trace and transfer the pumpkin template from page 115 and transfer it onto the aperture card. Cut out the aperture carefully using a craft knife and cutting mat.

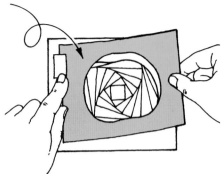

2 Turn the aperture over and line it up with the folding pattern on page 115. Use small pieces of masking tape to hold the aperture in place on top of the pattern. You can use the pattern directly from the page or photocopy or trace it first.

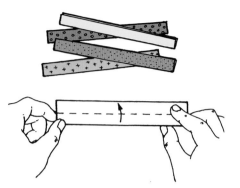

3 Place the rectangles of gift wrap sideways on, with the white side on top. Valley fold each one in half from bottom to top, as shown.

4 Cut each rectangle into 5cm (2in) strips and group them by colour. Number each group as follows: green 1, red 2, yellow 3 and orange 4.

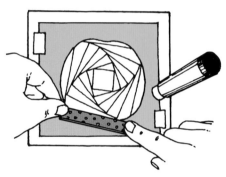

5 To begin iris folding, first apply a line of glue around the aperture, adjacent to section 1* of the folding pattern. Try not to smear any glue onto the pattern. Take a strip from group 1, position it exactly over section 1*, with its folded edge facing towards the middle and glue in place.

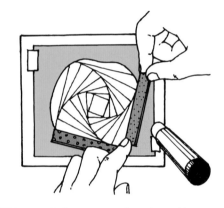

6 Take a strip from group 2 and, working anti-clockwise, place it over the pattern's outer section marked with a 2, and glue in place. Repeat with strips from groups 3 and 4, positioning and gluing them in place over sections 3 and 4 respectively. You have made one 'round' of the pattern.

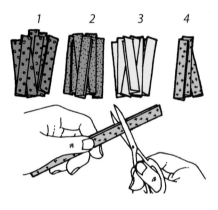

7 Start the next round with a strip from group 1, applying glue to the previous strip when you stick the next one in place.

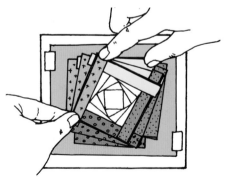

8 Continue working anti-clockwise around the folding pattern, taking a strip from each of the four groups in turn and making one full round each time until you reach the middle.

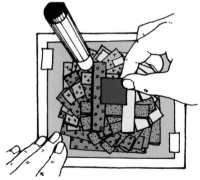

9 Glue the dark purple square over the central hole.

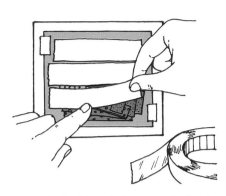

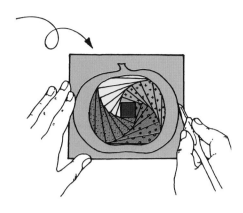

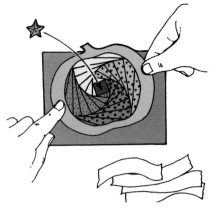

10 Apply double-sided tape to the back of the iris folding, as shown, to hold all the strips in place.

11 Gently remove the iris folding from the pattern and turn it over to reveal the folding in its aperture. Carefully cut around the pumpkin's outer edge, cutting through all layers as one.

12 To complete the card, attach the star sticker at the design's centre. Remove the backing from the strips of double-sided tape on the back of the pumpkin and carefully mount it centrally on the rectangle of black craft card.

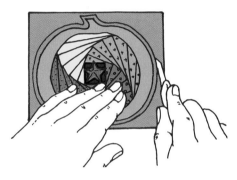

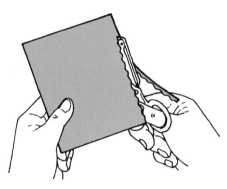

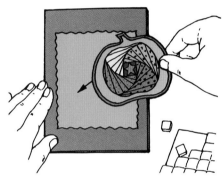

13 Echoing the pumpkin's shape, trim the black craft card, leaving a border of approximately 0.2cm (¹⁄₁₆in).

14 Using the deckle-edged scissors, trim the remaining rectangle of orange craft card on all sides.

15 Apply double-sided tape to one surface of the orange card and mount it centrally on the front of the black two-panel card. Attach the pumpkin to the centre with adhesive foam pads.

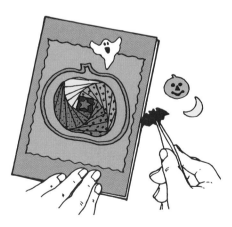

16 To finish, complete the decorations with Halloween theme stickers.

« Falling Leaves

Use the template and folding pattern on page 115 to make this elegant card. Stick a 21 x 5cm (8¼ x 2in) strip of burgundy card to a slightly wider strip of gold card and glue this to the centre of the two-panel card. Make the iris-folded leaf in the same way as for the pumpkin and glue this to a slightly larger piece of gold card. Stick this to the centre of your card and add gold peel-offs to finish.

Christening Shoes

A Christening is a wonderful time for giving gifts, and you'll want your special gift to be presented in the best possible way. This doesn't necessarily mean a fancy method of wrapping; these cute baby shoes will set off your gift to perfection. If you have a small gift, such as a bracelet, you could pop it inside one of the shoes. Otherwise attach the shoes to the outside of the wrapped gift.

You will need

✓ Two 21cm (8¼in) squares of pearlescent gift wrap

✓ Two 40cm (15¾in) lengths of 0.8cm (⁵⁄₁₆in) wide ribbon

✓ Two sticky-backed hearts with pearl centres

✓ Basic tool kit

At approximately 10cm (4in) long, these dinky baby shoes are the ideal decoration for a baby's present and can be hung up in the nursery after the gift has been opened or kept with other mementos of this precious time. Each shoe is made from a single square of pearlescent gift wrap and has a stick-on heart decoration, although you could use any type of sticker or small embellishment that you feel will provide the perfect finishing touch. The narrow ribbon trim not only adds further decoration but also keeps each shoe neatly closed.

Pink for a Girl »

These shoes were made from pink pearlescent gift wrap, pink ribbon and pink sticky-backed hearts for a girl; for a boy, use blue pearlescent paper (see above) and blue ribbon. However, you don't have to choose traditional colours. You could make them in yellow, in white with gold ribbon or simply select a paper that you like and choose the ribbon and stick-on embellishments to coordinate.

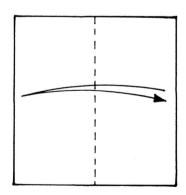

1 To make the shoe, fold and unfold a square of pearlescent gift wrap in half from right to left with the plain side on top.

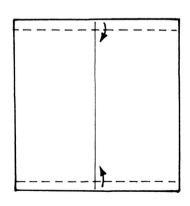

2 Valley fold the top and bottom edges over a little to make two coloured bands of paper that are equal in width.

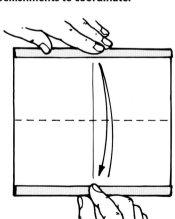

3 Fold and unfold in half from bottom to top, as shown.

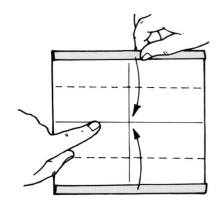

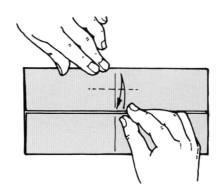

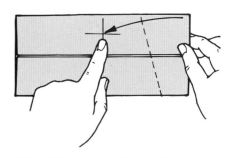

4 Valley fold the top and bottom edges in to meet the middle fold-line.

5 Valley fold the upper middle edge over to meet the top edge. Do not press the paper flat, but only mark it, as shown by the dashed lines. Return the middle edge to its original position.

6 Valley fold the top right-hand corner over to where the fold-lines intersect.

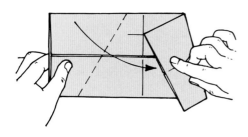

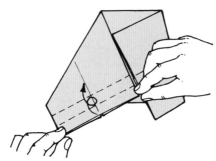

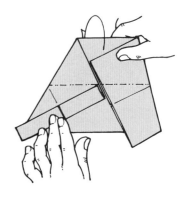

7 Valley fold the top left-hand corner and adjoining part of the top edge over to meet the right-hand sloping edge.

8 Valley fold the lower left-hand sloping edge over and over, as shown, to make a band of paper.

9 Mountain fold in half from top to bottom, as shown.

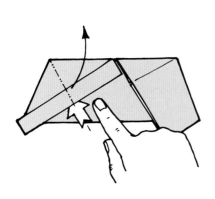

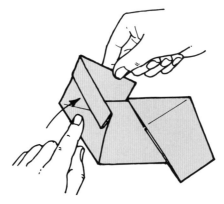

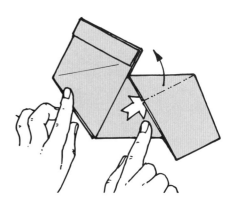

10 Lift the band of paper up, at the same time…

11 taking the adjoining section of paper with it.

12 Press flat into the position shown, making the shoe's heel. Lift the right-hand section of paper up, so that it lies along the heel's sloping edge, as shown in step 13, to make the toe.

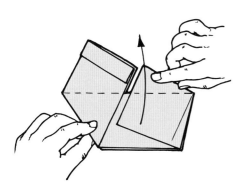

13 Valley fold the front section of paper up on a line between the two side points.

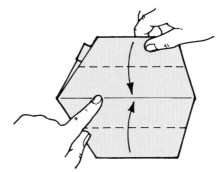

14 Valley fold the top and bottom edges in to meet middle fold-line.

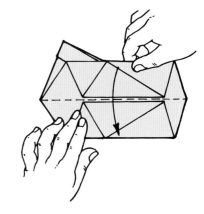

15 Valley fold in half from top to bottom.

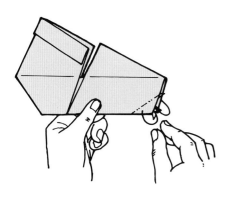

16 Mountain fold the toe's bottom corners up inside the model.

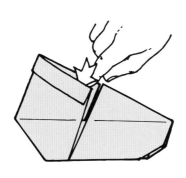

17 Insert your index finger inside the heel's back and open it out, making the model become three-dimensional.

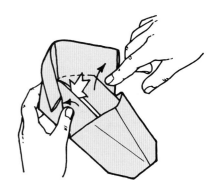

18 Lift the inner layers of paper out to each side to shape the shoe's toe.

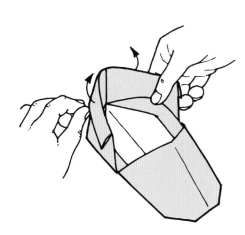

19 Unfold the heel's topmost band of paper, as shown.

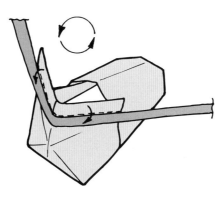

20 Place a length of ribbon around the heel so that it protrudes equally on each side of the model, as shown. Refold the heel's topmost band of paper, trapping the ribbon.

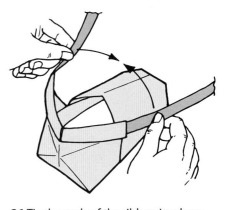

21 Tie the ends of the ribbon in a bow to hold the model together. Cut off any surplus ribbon at an angle. To finish, remove the backing from a sticky heart and attach it to the shoe just below the bow. Now make a second shoe by repeating steps 1 to 21 with the remaining square of pearlescent gift wrap, ribbon and sticky-backed heart.

Tulip Bouquet

Flowers bring life to a room and invigorate even the darkest area. Traditionally they were the method by which a lover could pass a secret message to his lady. A white camellia complimented the lady's perfect loveliness, honeysuckle promised fidelity while red tulips were a declaration of love. These distinctive flowers will last forever and make a beautiful keepsake in a decoratively wrapped container.

You will need

- ✓ Ten 10cm (4in) squares of green origami paper
- ✓ Ten 7cm (2¾in) squares of origami paper in a mixture of orange, pink, red and yellow
- ✓ Two 26cm (10¼in) squares of gold and wine-coloured gift wrap
- ✓ 60cm (23⅝in) length of raffia
- ✓ Cotton wool
- ✓ Ten 16cm (6⅜in) lengths of 20 gauge green covered florists' wire
- ✓ Green floral tape
- ✓ Block of oasis foam
- ✓ Plastic flowerpot about 8.5cm (3⅜in) in height and diameter
- ✓ Basic tool kit

You'll be using some of the techniques we've already covered to create these splendid tulips, and if you have made the yellow flower card shown on page 19 you'll be partway there. Each flower is mounted on a stem of florists' wire and has a long, elegant leaf wrapped into the stem a little way down. Just where you add the leaf and how you arrange the completed tulips in the pot is a matter for your own creativity, so let the artist in you emerge as you craft each flower and place it in the pot. Each finished tulip is approximately 19cm (7½in) long.

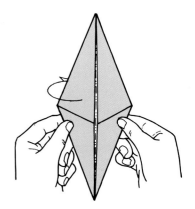

Beautiful Bouquet »

A bouquet of flowers is always a lovely gift, but this one is even more special because each bloom has been hand crafted and will last forever. With this gift you show that you have not only chosen something of beauty but have taken the time and effort to create it yourself. No two bouquets will be the same so your gift will be unique.

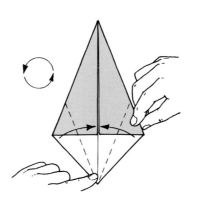

1 To make the leaves, repeat steps 12 and 13 for the daffodil tea bag card on page 21 with one square of green origami paper. Turn the kite base around into the position shown. From the bottom point, valley fold the sloping edges in to meet the middle fold-line, making a diamond base.

2 Mountain fold the diamond base in half from left to right.

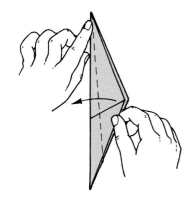

3 From the top point, valley fold the front flap of paper over to the left on a slant.

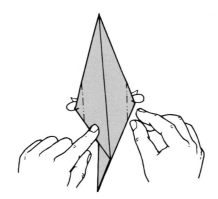

4 Mountain fold a little of each side point behind. To finish, press the paper flat. Repeat steps 1 to 4 with the remaining nine squares of green origami paper.

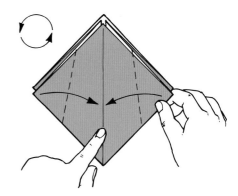

5 To make the tulips, repeat steps 1 to 7 for the yellow flower card on pages 22–23 with one square of tulip-coloured origami paper. Turn the preliminary fold around so that the open layers are pointing away from you. Valley fold the top side points in to meet the middle fold-line on a slant.

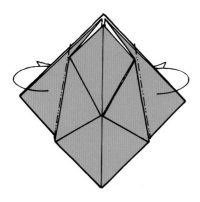

6 Mountain fold the bottom side points behind to meet the middle fold-line on a slant, as shown.

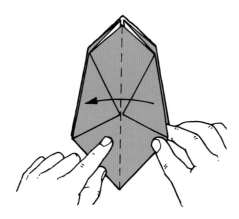

7 Valley fold the top right-hand flap over to the left.

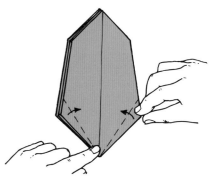

8 From the bottom point, valley fold over a little of the lower sloping edges.

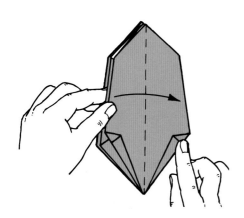

9 Valley fold two left-hand flaps over to the right.

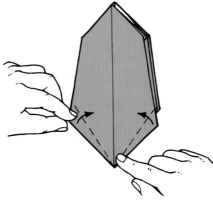

10 From the bottom point, valley fold over a little of the lower sloping edges.

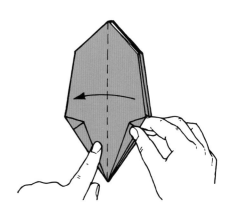

11 Valley fold the top right-hand flap over to the left.

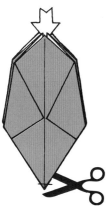

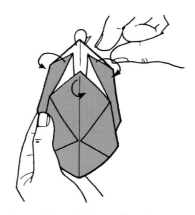

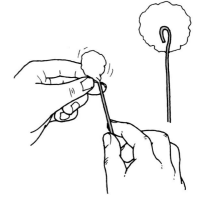

12 Snip off the bottom point to make a tiny hole. Open out the top points, making the tulip become three-dimensional.

13 Softly curl the tulip's petals with your fingers to curve them outwards.

14 Using the pliers, bend a small hook into one end of a length of florists' wire. Little by little, wrap small amounts of cotton wool around the hook, making a pompom that is approximately 1cm (³⁄₈in) in diameter.

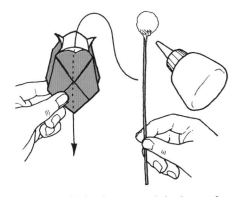

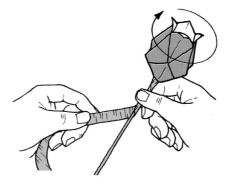

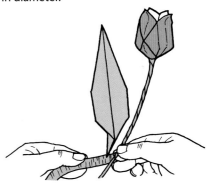

15 Place a little glue around the base of the pompom. Insert the wire's bottom end into the tulip and out through the hole. Pull the wire down until the pompom's glued area attaches itself to the inside of the tulip at the bottom.

16 Gently stretch a length of green floral tape to release the impregnated adhesive. Beginning at the hole end of the tulip, wrap the tape around the wire a few times. Now slant the tape at a downward angle and wind it spirally down, covering the wire by rotating the tulip.

17 At the required point, tape a leaf into place. Try to take in just a fraction of the leaf's stem as you are taping. Continue rotating the tulip and taping until the entire length of wire is covered. This finishes one tulip. Repeat steps 5 to 17 to make nine more tulips.

18 To assemble the bouquet, use the craft knife to cut the block of oasis foam to fit inside the plastic flowerpot. Arrange the tulips in the oasis foam. There are no hard and fast rules – flower arranging depends on personal taste and preference.

19 Place the two squares of gift wrap together, plain sides on top. Slightly rotate the upper sheet, as shown. With the tulip arrangement in their centre, bring the gift wrap layers up around the flowerpot.

20 Arrange the folds of the gift wrap into a ruffle. Place a length of raffia around the ruffle and tie its ends together in a bow, holding the pot and ruffle together.

Kirigami Album Cover

Here is a Japanese paper-cutting technique known as kirigami. If you have ever made snowflakes at school by folding paper, snipping away portions and then unfolding the paper to reveal a lacy pattern, you have already tried this appealing technique. Here we show you how you can use it to create flowers, petals, snowflakes and spider's webs and how to put your creations to good use decorating an album cover and greetings cards.

You will need

For the photo album

✓ Twelve 4cm (1⅝in) squares of handmade paper in various shades of pink (eight squares for the cherry blossom and four for the petals)

✓ 10cm (4in) square of pink handmade paper for the heart base

✓ Photograph album, approximately 25cm (10in) square, covered with handmade paper

✓ Eight small pink pearl beads

✓ Two 30cm (12in) lengths of 0.5cm (¼in) wide pink ribbon

✓ Basic tool kit

The decorations shown here are based on a five-fold or six-fold, which can be used to make an exact pentagon or hexagon. Instructions for making these useful folds are given at the beginning of each project, and you can practice them first on a 15cm (6in) square of origami paper if you wish. Once you have mastered the folding you can go on to make the decorations using the patterns provided, or invent your own shapes to cut from the folded paper. Experimentation will show you which shapes work well, but be sure to position them on the folded paper in the same way as the shapes given here. If you compare the blossom and petal diagrams on page 91 you will see how even a slight adjustment to your cutting pattern can have a dramatic effect.

« Cards

Kirigami is ideal for making all sorts of symmetrical decorations. Here the technique has been used to make snowflakes and spider's webs to decorate themed cards. For instructions, see pages 92–93. When cutting the folded paper make sure you hold the layers together and keep in mind which point is the centre of the design.

Wedding Album »

Special photographs deserve to be housed in a beautiful album like this one. It's based on a ready-made album covered in a fairly plain handmade paper, which has been decorated with a heart covered in paper flowers. A small ribbon bow and scattering of paper petals complete the look. You could also use this idea to decorate a Valentine's Day card.

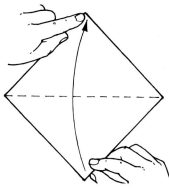

1 To make a five-fold, turn the square of origami paper around to look like a diamond, with the white side on top. Valley fold in half from bottom to top, making a diaper fold.

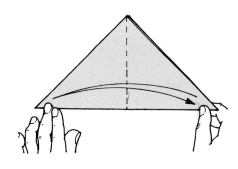

2 Fold and unfold in half from right to left.

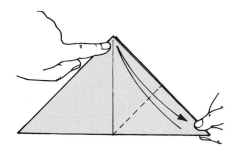

3 Valley fold the bottom right-hand point up to meet the top point. Press flat and unfold.

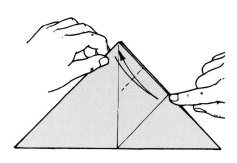

4 Valley fold top point down to where the fold-line made in step 3 connects with the right-hand sloping edge. Be careful to press the paper only as shown by the dashed lines. Unfold.

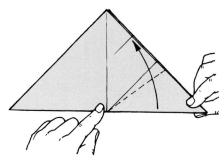

5 Valley fold the right-hand half of the bottom edge up to where the fold-line made in step 4 connects with the right-hand sloping edge.

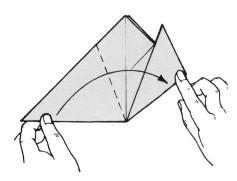

6 Valley fold the left-hand half of the bottom edge over to lie along the lower right-hand sloping edge.

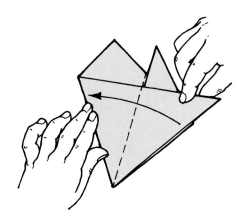

7 Valley fold the front flap of paper in half from right to left.

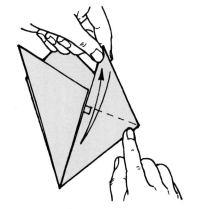

8 Staring at the right-hand side point, valley fold the top right-hand point down, so that the fold-line hits the middle edges at ninety degrees. Press flat and unfold.

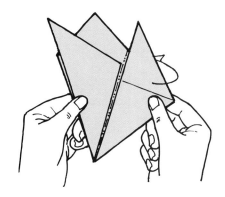

9 Mountain fold in half from right to left, finishing the five-fold.

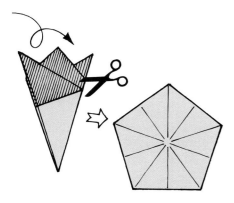

10 To make a pentagon, turn the paper over. Cut along the fold-line made in step 8 and discard the parts that are shaded in the diagram. Carefully unfold the remaining piece of paper to reveal a pentagon.

11 To make the cherry blossom, repeat steps 1 to 9 with one square of pink handmade paper. Turn the paper over. Using the pencil, copy the blossom's pattern onto the five-fold, as shown. Cut away and discard the parts that are shaded in the diagram. Carefully unfold the remaining pieces of paper to reveal the cherry blossom. Repeat this step with a further seven squares.

12 To make the petals, repeat steps 1 to 9 with one square of pink handmade paper. Turn the paper over. Using the pencil, copy the petal's pattern onto the five-fold, as shown. Cut away and discard the parts that are shaded in the diagram. Carefully unfold the remaining pieces of paper to reveal the petals. Repeat this step with the remaining three squares.

13 To make the heart base, trace the base template from page 117 onto its square of pink handmade paper. Using the scissors, carefully cut around the solid black line and discard the excess paper.

14 Arrange and glue the cherry blossoms onto the heart base so that they are closely packed together, leaving hardly any noticeable space. Glue a small pink pearl bead into the centre of each blossom, as shown.

15 Glue the back of the heart base centrally onto the front of the photograph album. Place the lengths of ribbon one on top of the other and tie them together in a double bow. Attach the bow to the album with double-sided tape, just above the heart base.

16 To finish, arrange the petals on the album's upper right- and lower left-hand corners as if they were swirling around in a light breeze. When you are satisfied with the arrangement, glue them in place.

Cherry Blossom »
Cherry blossom has a very short lifespan and can be swept away by the breeze, but you can retain the fleeting beauty of this flower by making your own, and in doing so create a valued family memento.

You will need

For the snowflake card

✓ Dark blue two-panel card

✓ 7.5cm (3in) square of thin white paper for a snowflake

✓ 7.5cm (3in) square of thin silver gift wrap for a snowflake

✓ 5 x 15cm (2 x 6in) piece of white pearlescent craft card

✓ Crystal glitter glue

✓ Themed stickers

✓ Adhesive foam pads

✓ Basic tool kit

« Icy Landscape

Here's a simple decorative idea for a Christmas card that makes a feature of six-fold snowflakes. It's quick to construct using craft card, themed stickers and glitter glue for a seasonal background that sets off the paper shapes. There's also a Halloween card to make, shown opposite.

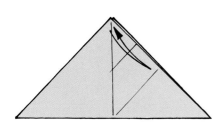

1 To make a six-fold, repeat steps 1 to 4 of the five-fold on page 90 with the square of origami paper.

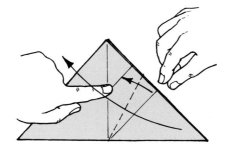

2 From the middle of the bottom edge, valley fold the bottom right-hand point up so that the sloping fold-line connects with the fold mark, as shown.

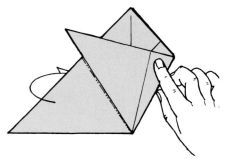

3 Mountain fold the left-hand half of the bottom edge behind so that it lies along the right-hand sloping edge.

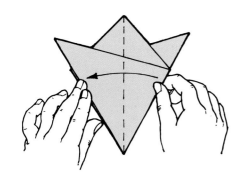

4 Valley fold in half from right to left, finishing the six-fold.

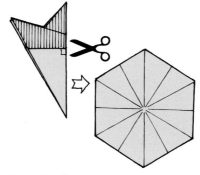

5 To make a hexagon, cut across the paper from right to left in a straight line, making sure that the start of the cut is at ninety degrees to the right-hand edge. Discard the parts that are shaded in the diagram. Carefully unfold the remaining piece of paper to reveal a hexagon.

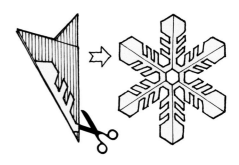

6 To make the snowflakes, repeat steps 1 to 4 for the six-fold with both snowflake squares of paper. Trace and transfer the snowflake template from page 116 onto the six-folds. Cut away and discard the parts that are shaded in the diagram. Carefully unfold the remaining pieces of paper to reveal the snowflakes.

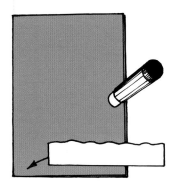

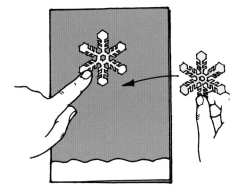

7 For the snowflake card, place the white pearlescent craft card sideways on. Cut a series of waves along its top edge, suggesting a snowy landscape. Glue it onto the front of the dark blue two-panel card, aligning their bottom edges and sides.

8 Glue both snowflakes, the silver one slightly over the white one, onto the front of the two-panel card, as shown.

9 Decorate the card with Christmas themed stickers, attaching the crystal fir trees with adhesive foam pads. To finish, complete the decorations with dabs of crystal glitter glue to suggest falling snow.

Halloween Card

You will need

For the Halloween card

- ✓ Black two-panel card
- ✓ 7.5cm (3in) square of thin white paper for the small web
- ✓ 12cm (4¾in) square of thin gold gift wrap for the large web
- ✓ Small plastic toy spider with a 15cm (6in) length of gold thread attached to its body
- ✓ Themed stickers
- ✓ Adhesive foam pads
- ✓ Basic tool kit

« Halloween Spiders
The spider's web is a little more complicated than the snowflake and you will need to use a craft knife to cut it out neatly. We've made two for this spooky card, one large and one small. (See pages 76–79 for some more Halloween cards.)

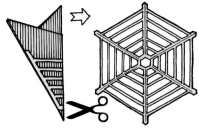

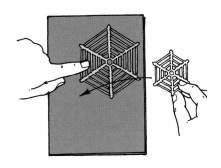

1 To make the spider's webs, repeat steps 1 to 4 for the snowflake card with both web squares of paper. Trace and transfer the web templates from page 116 onto their respective six-folds. Cut away and discard the parts that are shaded in the diagram. Unfold the remaining pieces of paper to reveal the webs.

2 For the Halloween card, glue both webs, the white one slightly over the gold one, onto the front of the black two-panel card, as shown.

3 Attach the spider and its thread to the right-hand side of the card with adhesive foam pads. Place a ghost sticker on the thread's foam pad to hide it. To finish, complete the decorations with Halloween theme stickers, attaching a few with adhesive foam pads to raise them up.

Christmas Star

Here is a simple way to make a decorative woven star from paper strips. The basic design was credited to Friedrich Froebel, a 19th century German educationalist, best known for creating what we still call kindergarten. Traditionally the stars were dipped in paraffin wax, sprinkled with glitter and hung on the Christmas tree, but they also make excellent decorations for wrapped gifts or original gift tags.

You will need

✓ A4 (21 x 29.5cm / 8¼ x 11⅝in) sheet of gift wrap or duo paper
✓ Gold thread for hanging
✓ Basic tool kit

This lovely star is made from four long strips of paper that are woven and folded. It's quite straightforward if you follow the steps carefully and cut the strips accurately. The instructions provided are to make a star approximately 7.5 x 7.5cm (3 x 3in), which will fit neatly on a card or gift. If you wish to make a larger or smaller star you can adjust the size of the strips, making sure that they are at least 15 times as long as they are wide. If in doubt, cut them longer than needed because you can always trim off the excess when the star is completed. For example, if you wish to use 3cm (1¼in) wide strips, they will need to be 45cm (17¾in) long. You may also wish to experiment with other types of paper. Paper ribbon works particularly well, and you will also have good results using some of the duo papers.

« Gift Toppers
To use the star to decorate a gift, simply omit the gold thread. The star will add a fabulous flourish to any gift that is wrapped with imagination and love, and will provide the unique look you desire.

Stars of Wonder »
These stunning Christmas ornaments are each made from four strips of ordinary gift wrap. Look out for festive colours such as red, green or gold in a fairly good quality paper that is strong enough to be woven. This model has been given other names over the years including The Star of Bethlehem.

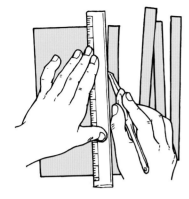

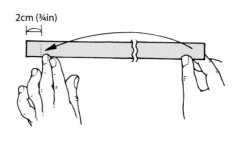

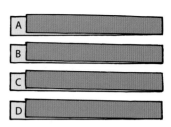

1 Place the sheet of gift wrap lengthways on, with the plain side on top. Cut four strips 2cm (¾in) wide.

2 Place a strip sideways on, with the plain side on top. Valley fold its right-hand side over to a point that is 2cm (¾in) from the left-hand side. Repeat with the remaining three strips.

3 As a guide during the folding, use the pencil to label the strips A, B, C and D.

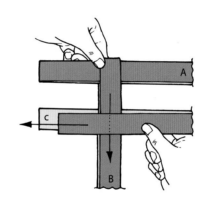

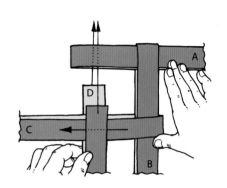

4 Take strips A and B and insert A between the layers of B, as shown.

5 Insert strip B between the layers of strip C. Slide strip C to the left.

6 Insert strip C between the layers of strip D, then insert strip D between the layers of strip A.

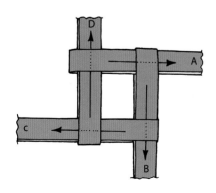

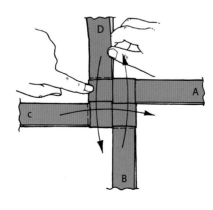

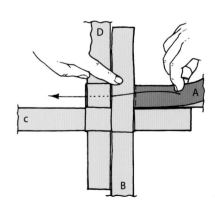

7 Carefully pull the strips in the directions shown, making a paper knot.

8 Working anti-clockwise, valley fold the top layers of strips D, C and B over the knot, as shown.

9 Valley fold the top layer of strip A over the knot, while at the same time taking great care to weave its end through.

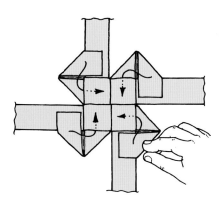

10 Pull the strip through, as shown. You should now have four short strips and four long ones.

11 Mountain fold the short strips diagonally behind, as shown.

12 Valley fold the short strips diagonally over, as shown.

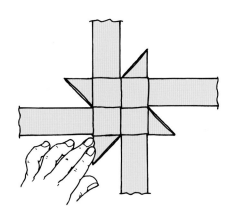

13 Valley fold the short strips inwards, inserting their ends inside the body of the knot, as shown.

14 You have now made four of the triangular points of the star.

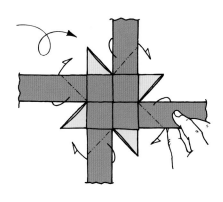

15 Turn the paper over. Mountain fold the long strips diagonally behind, as shown.

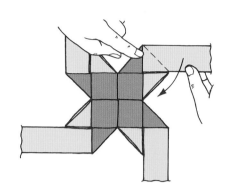

16 Valley fold one long strip diagonally over, as shown.

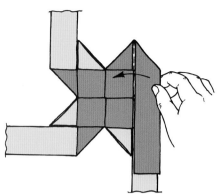

17 Valley fold the strip inwards, making a triangular point.

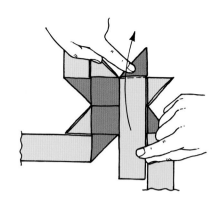

18 Valley fold the strip up over the point.

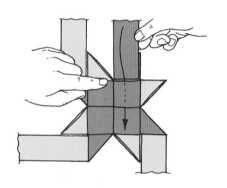

19 Being very careful not to tear the strip, weave its end through the knot.

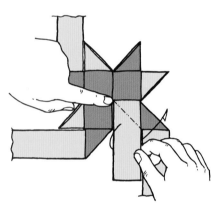

20 Mountain fold the strip diagonally behind, as shown.

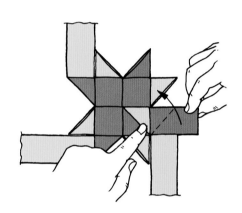

21 Valley fold the strip diagonally over.

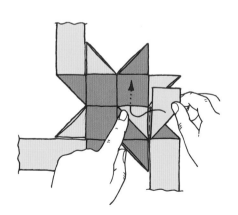

22 Valley fold the strip inwards, inserting its end inside the body of the knot, making a triangular point.

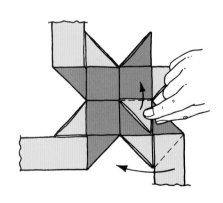

23 Valley fold the point over. Repeat steps 16 to 23 with the remaining three long strips.

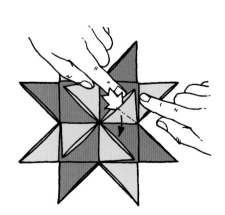

24 Open out one point and . . .

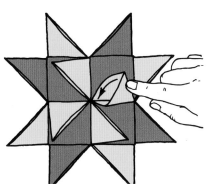

25 press it down neatly into a diamond.

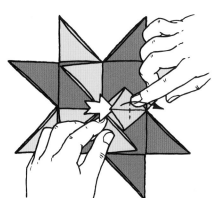

26 Open out the diamond, so that it becomes three-dimensional.

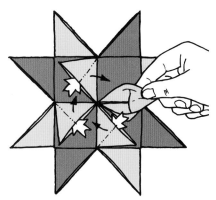

27 Repeat steps 24 to 26 with the remaining three points.

28 You have now finished the Christmas star.

29 Attach a loop of gold thread to the star, so that you can hang it from a Christmas tree, if desired.

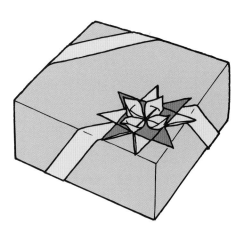

30 For a gift box decoration, omit the gold thread and use double-sided tape to fix the star in place.

Mother's Day Flower Ball

This masterpiece of origami looks incredibly impressive and complicated and would make a sophisticated Mother's Day present that will be treasured for a long, long time. It's actually made as a series of identical single-flower units that are tied together, and you'll find the process of folding each piece and then joining them together both enjoyable and therapeutic.

You will need

✓ Thirty-six 15cm (6in) squares of purple and lavender duo paper

✓ Two 70cm (27½in) lengths of 0.5cm (¼in) wide purple ribbon for the tail

✓ Two 70cm (27½in) lengths of 0.5cm (¼in) wide light green ribbon for the tail

✓ 60cm (23⅝in) length of 0.5cm (¼in) wide light green ribbon for the handle

✓ Pink foilart flowers

✓ Needle and strong sewing cotton

✓ Basic tool kit

This lovely flower ball is approximately 15.5cm (6⅛in) across. It is made up of 36 identical flower units that are strung together in groups of nine. The four groups are then tied together, incorporating the ribbon tails and handles, and the finished ball completed with a few pretty foilart decorations. You'll find that the more flowers you complete the quicker and more professional you become at making them, and soon you'll be constructing them with just a few glances at the step-by-step illustrations. Make sure you use duo paper that has nicely coordinating colours on each side because both sides have an important role in the look of the finished flower ball.

« Bridesmaid's Posy
We made this flower ball from pink and pearl duo paper trimmed with pink and opal ribbons and pearl foilart flowers for a bridesmaid's version. To make this version follow the instructions for the Mother's Day flower ball, treating the pearl side as the right side (lavender side).

Purple Haze »
Made from purple and lavender duo paper, this flower ball is a vision of elegance and will make a treasured gift for even the most discerning of mothers or grandmothers. There are many other colour combinations that would work really well too, such as white and gold, or two shades of the recipient's favourite colour.

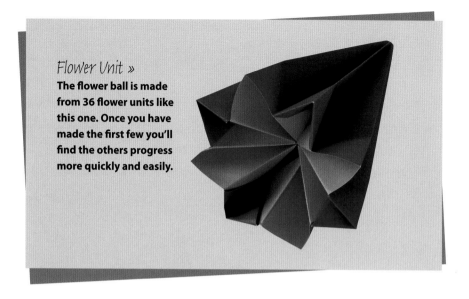

Flower Unit »
The flower ball is made from 36 flower units like this one. Once you have made the first few you'll find the others progress more quickly and easily.

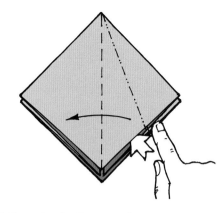

1 To make the flower units, repeat steps 1 to 7 for the yellow flower card on pages 22–23 with one square of duo paper, but with the purple side on top in step 1. Lift the top right-hand flap of paper.

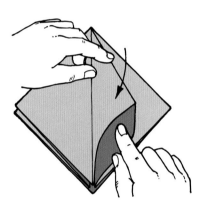

2 Open out the flap.

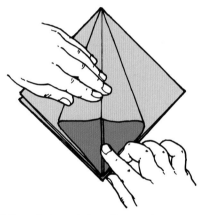

3 Press it down into a diamond.

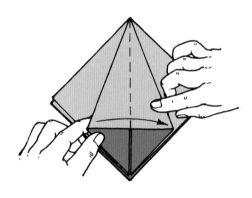

4 Valley fold the diamond in half from left to right.

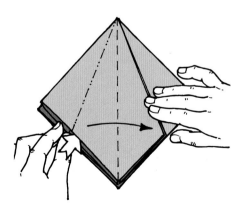

5 Repeat steps 1 to 3 with the top left-hand flap of paper.

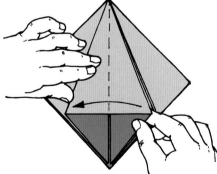

6 Valley fold the diamond in half from right to left, like turning a page of a book.

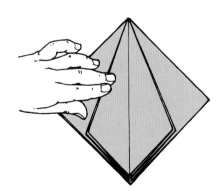

7 Press the paper flat.

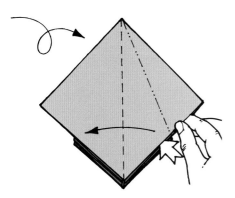

8 Turn the paper over. Repeat steps 1 to 7.

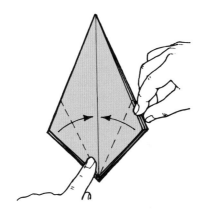

9 Valley fold the front flap's lower sloping edges in to meet the middle fold-line.

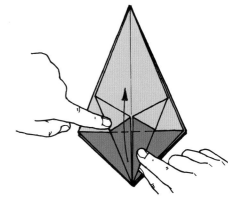

10 Valley fold the front point as far as it will go.

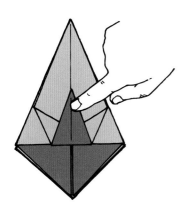

11 Press the point down.

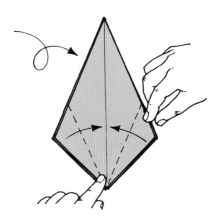

12 Turn the paper over. Now repeat steps 9 to 11.

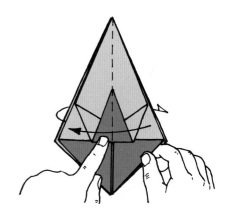

13 Find the remaining two front flaps by opening the layers of paper like the pages of a book.

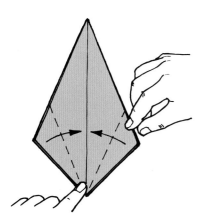

14 Now repeat steps 9 to 12 on the remaining flaps.

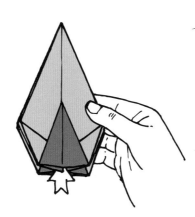

15 This should be the result. Press the paper flat. Now open it out completely.

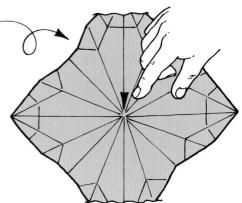

16 Turn the paper over so that the lavender side is on top. Press down on the paper's middle, making it become bowl-like in appearance.

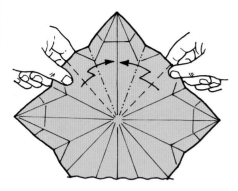

17 Position the paper as shown. Starting with the top point and using the existing valley and mountain fold-lines, take the middle of the top right and left edges behind to the middle.

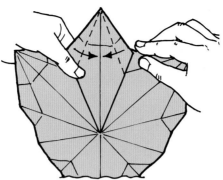

18 Valley fold the sloping edges in to meet the middle fold-line.

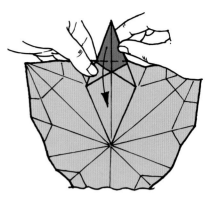

19 Valley fold the top point down along the line of the horizontal edge.

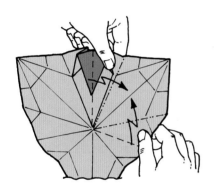

20 Take the middle of the right-hand corner's two edges behind, in effect repeating step 17. Now repeat steps 18 and 19.

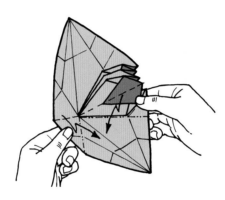

21 Repeat steps 17 to 19 with what was originally the bottom point.

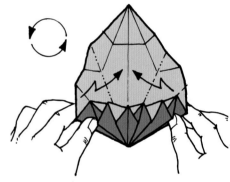

22 Turn the paper around to the position shown. Repeat step 17 with what was originally the left-hand corner.

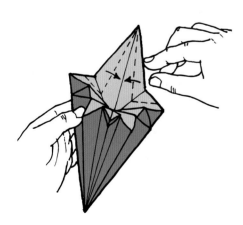

23 Repeat step 18.

24 Valley fold the point down, tucking it into the model to complete one unit. Repeat steps 1 to 24 with the remaining thirty-five squares.

Make a total of 36 units like this one.

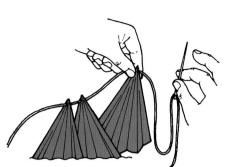

25 To assemble the flower ball, pass a length of strong cotton through the base of nine units.

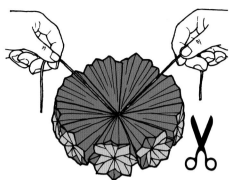

26 Tie the ends of the cotton together, in a double knot, completing one cluster of flowers. Cut off any surplus cotton. Now make three more clusters.

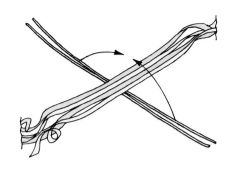

27 Cut two 40cm (15¾in) lengths of cotton and place them together side by side. Lay the tail ribbons over the lengths of cotton, as shown. Tie the lengths of cotton around the ribbons' middle into a double knot.

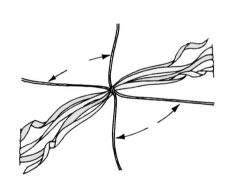

28 Carefully separate the lengths of cotton into the letter X, as shown.

29 Place one cluster on top of the X. Tie opposite lengths of cotton together into a double knot.

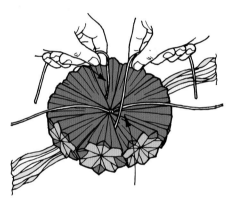

30 Tie the remaining lengths of cotton together into a double knot.

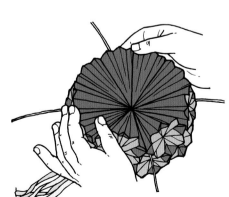

31 Place a second cluster on top. Tie opposite lengths of cotton together into a double knot. Now repeat step 30.

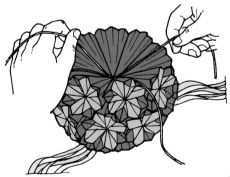

32 Repeat step 31 with the remaining two clusters.

33 Lay the ribbon for the handle over the lengths of cotton, as shown.

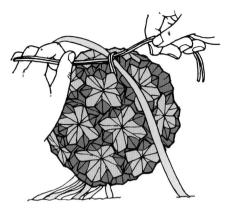

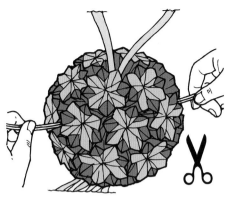

34 Hold each of the two lengths of cotton together and tie a loose knot around the ribbon, while at the same time gently pulling it down into the clusters.

35 When the ribbon cannot go any further, fasten the knot tightly. Tie another knot on top, securing everything together and making the clusters become a round ball. Finally, cut off any surplus cotton.

36 Tie the ends of the ribbon handle into a bow.

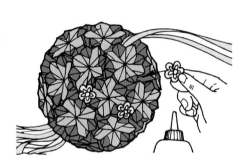

37 Add extra sparkle by gluing the foilart flowers around the ball.

38 To finish, curl the tail's ribbons over the closed blades of a pair of scissors.

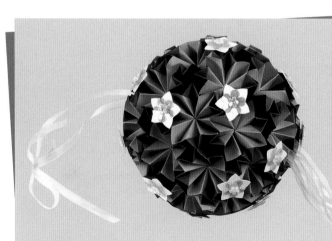

« Shimmering Finish
Foil art flowers are the perfect quick finishing touch, but if preferred you can punch paper shapes from metallic paper, decorate them with beads and glitter, and glue these on instead.

Bridesmaid's Posy »
This posy is embellished with glittering ribbons and foil art flowers to catch the sunlight and win the hearts of many a bridesmaid. If desired, add essential oil using an eye dropper to heighten the impact of the flower ball.

Teddy Bear Gift Tag

The right gift tag can be the making of a gift and if it is sufficiently attractive can form the centerpiece of the wrapping. This cute teddy bear is an excellent example, and looks wonderful with a plain wrapping or a wrapping that has been decorated with a simple motif, from, say, a craft stamp. Children will love it, and if you pop the bear in a plain envelope you can include a secret message, an age badge or other small birthday trinket.

You will need

✓ Two 15cm (6in) squares of brown origami paper

✓ 3 x 6cm (1³⁄₁₆ x 2³⁄₈in) piece of blue gift wrap for the bow tie

✓ 20cm (8in) length of 0.8cm (⁵⁄₁₆in) wide blue ribbon

✓ Three 0.8cm (⁵⁄₁₆in) diameter black circular peel-offs

✓ Black felt-tip pen

✓ Blue sticky-backed gem heart

✓ Basic tool kit

We love to break down complicated folding shapes into units because it makes them so much easier to complete, and this teddy bear gift tag is no exception. It's made in three parts. The head and body are made separately and then glued together, while the bow, which comes from the tuxedo gift bag (see page 50), is added on top. The eyes and nose are simple round black peel-offs and the mouth is drawn on with a pen, but if you can find sticky dots in different colours you could change the colours of the eyes to match those of the child. You could even use sticky-backed google eyes, which most kids love.

« Girl's Bear
This endearing bear is made from light brown origami paper and has a bow made from pink gingham gift wrap with a pink ribbon tie and pink sticky-backed gem heart. It's bound to delight any small girl. The finished bear is 13cm (5in) tall and 9cm (3½in) wide.

Bearing Gifts »
Made from just two 15cm (6in) squares of origami paper plus a strip of gift wrap for the bow, this bear is inexpensive to make but a delight to receive. Plain origami paper is relatively easy to get hold of and works well here but you could use patterned paper if preferred (see page 113) or try ordinary brown wrapping paper, which is the perfect bear colour.

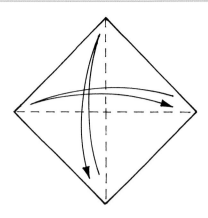

1 To make the body, turn one square of origami paper around so that it looks like a diamond, with the white side on top. Valley fold the opposite corners together in turn to mark the diagonal fold-lines, then open up again.

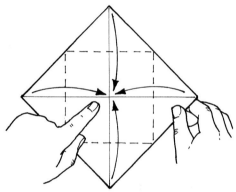

2 Valley fold the corners in to the middle, as shown…

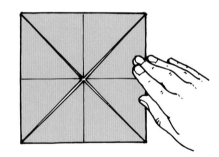

3 making a blintz base.

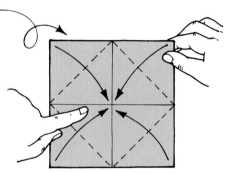

4 Turn the base over. Valley fold the corners in to the middle.

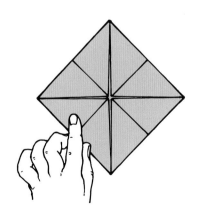

5 Press the paper flat.

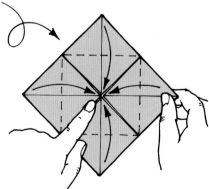

6 Turn the paper over. Once again, valley fold the corners in to the middle.

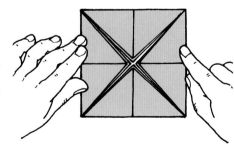

7 Press the paper flat.

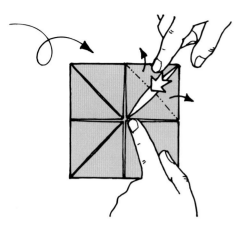

8 Turn the paper over. Open out one corner square.

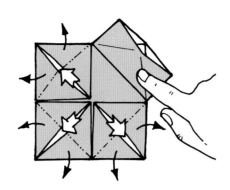

9 Press the corner down neatly into a rectangle. Repeat with the remaining three corner squares.

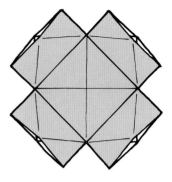

10 This should be your result. Press the paper flat.

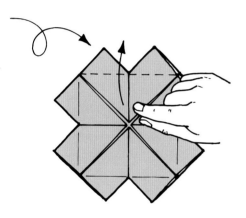

11 Turn the paper over. Valley fold one middle point out, as shown.

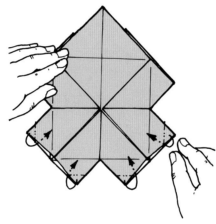

12 Inside reverse fold a little of each lower rectangles' side points.

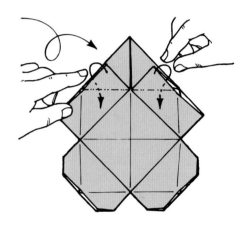

13 Turn the paper over. Along the existing horizontal fold-lines, inside reverse fold the top right- and left-hand side points.

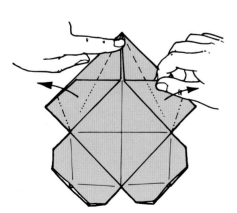

14 Pull out the top right- and left-hand pockets.

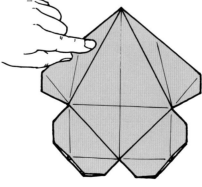

15 Press them down neatly to each side, as shown. This finishes the body.

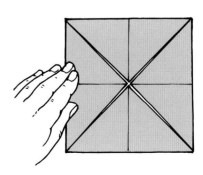

16 To make the head, repeat steps 1 and 2 for the body with the remaining square of origami paper.

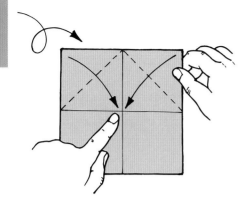

17 Turn the paper over. Valley fold the top corners in to the middle.

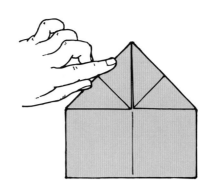

18 Press the paper flat.

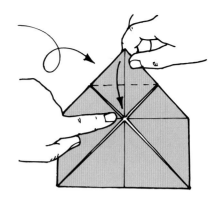

19 Turn the paper over. Valley fold the top point in to the middle.

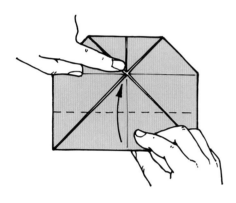

20 Valley fold the bottom edge up to meet the adjacent horizontal fold-line.

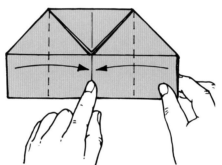

21 Valley fold the sides in to meet the middle line.

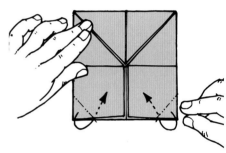

22 Inside reverse fold a little of each bottom corner.

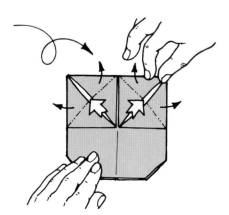

23 Turn the paper over. Open out the corner squares and press them down neatly into rectangles.

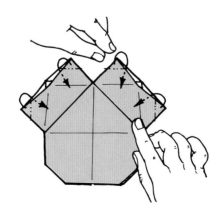

24 Inside reverse fold a little of each rectangle's side points. This finishes the head.

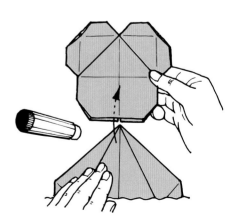

25 To assemble the bear, insert and glue the body's top point between the head's lower layers, as shown.

26 Using the black felt-tip pen, draw on the bear's mouth, as shown. Remove the backing from the peel-offs and attach them to the face for the eyes and nose.

27 Repeat steps 12 and 13 for the stocking card on page 59 with the hole punch and the length of blue ribbon.

28 Repeat steps 1 to 8 for the tuxedo gift bag on page 54 with the piece of blue gift wrap. Apply glue to the back of the finished bow tie and mount it on the bear, just under its chin.

29 To finish, remove the backing from the gem heart and attach it to the bear's body, just below the bow, as shown.

Golden Bear »
For this variation we used golden brown polka dot paper with red polka dot gift wrap for the bow tie and a red sticky-back gem heart – ideal to make a child go dotty with delight.

Templates and Folding Patterns

Owl Template (see page 76)

Aperture line

Outer edge

Owl/Bat Folding Pattern (see page 76)

Starting point

Bat Template (see page 76)

Aperture line

Outer edge

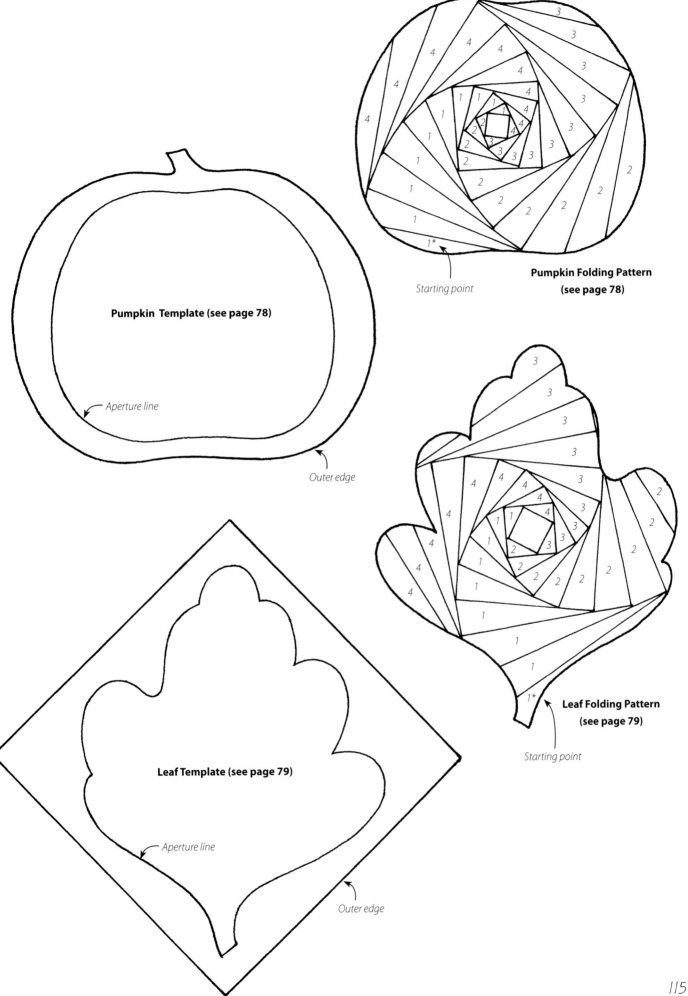

Pumpkin Template (see page 78)

Aperture line

Outer edge

3
3
3
4 4 4
4
1 1 1
4
4
1 1 4
4
1 2 2 4 4
1 2 3 3 3
1 2 3 3 3 3
1 2 3 3
1 2 2 3
1 2 2
1 2 2 2
1 2 2
1 2 2
1
1*

Starting point

**Pumpkin Folding Pattern
(see page 78)**

3
3
3
3
3
3
4 4 4 2
4 4 3 2
4 1 4 2
4 1 4 2
4 1 2 3 3 2 2
4 1 2 2 2 2
1 2 2
1
1
1
1*

**Leaf Folding Pattern
(see page 79)**

Starting point

Leaf Template (see page 79)

Aperture line

Outer edge

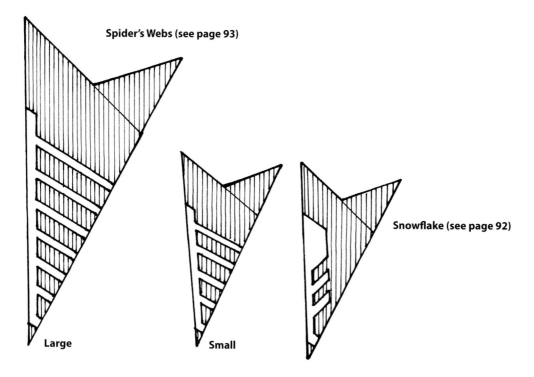

Spider's Webs (see page 93)

Snowflake (see page 92)

Large

Small

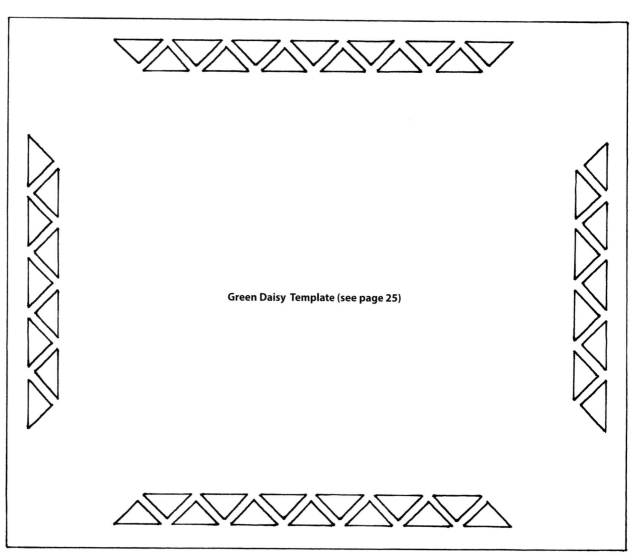

Green Daisy Template (see page 25)

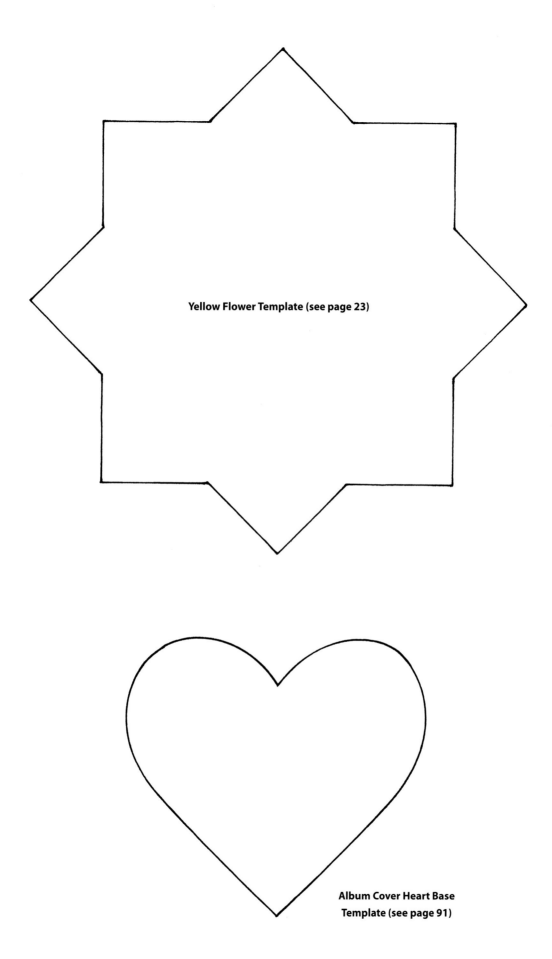

Yellow Flower Template (see page 23)

Album Cover Heart Base
Template (see page 91)

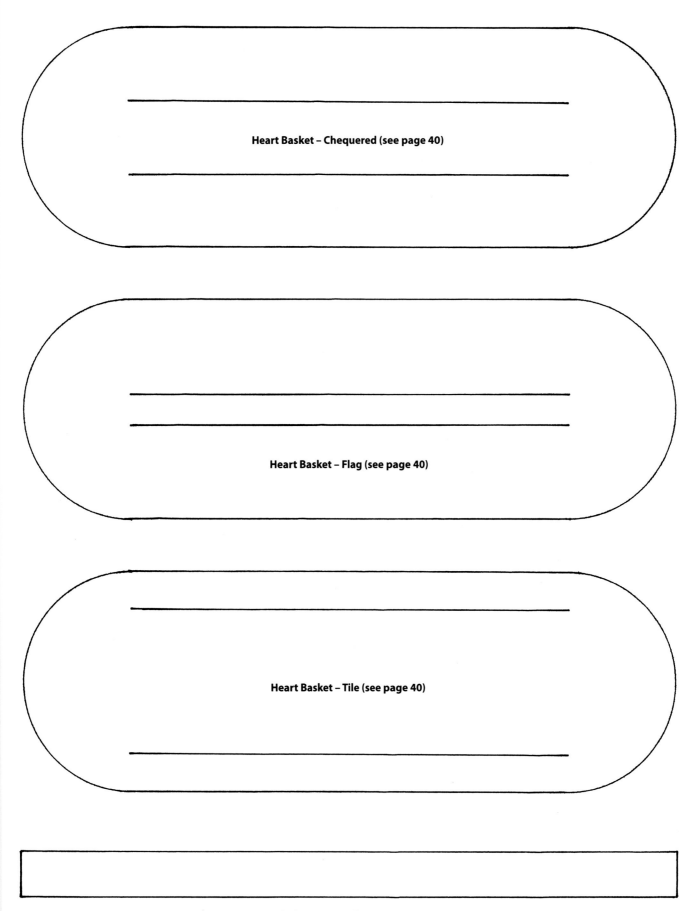

Heart Basket – Chequered (see page 40)

Heart Basket – Flag (see page 40)

Heart Basket – Tile (see page 40)

Handle for Heart Baskets (see page 40)

Resources

The best approach for gathering the materials you require for paper crafting is to keep on the lookout and build up gradually over time. Your local craft shop can order a particular product for you, give advice about your purchases, should you require it, and may offer regular craft clubs and workshops. The Internet gives access to a wider choice of suppliers from all over the world. Here are the details of a few suppliers to get you started.

United Kingdom

Book Ends
25/28 Thurloe Place
South Kensington
London SW7 2HQ
tel: 020 7589 2285
email: bookend@beconnect.com
Specialists in paper crafts, origami paper and many other craft products.

Creativity Cards and Crafts
5/6 The Labyrinth
7 Mark Lane
Eastbourne
East Sussex BN21 4RJ
tel/fax: 01323 439769
A craft shop and studio dedicated to paper crafts. Supplier of embellishments, peel-offs, tea bag and kaleidoscope papers and other sundry items.

Craftzone
10A Britannia Works
Skinner Lane
Pontefract
West Yorkshire WF8 1NA
tel: 01977 699888
www.craftzone.pwp.blueyonder.co.uk
Card making and general craft retailer.

Falkiner Fine Papers
76 Southampton Row
London WC1B 4AR
tel: 020 7831 1151
fax: 020 7430 1248
email: falkiner@ic24.net
Handmade paper suppler. Mail order service.

Japan Centre
212 Piccadilly
London W1J 9HG
tel: 020 7439 8035
fax: 020 7287 1082
email: info@japancentrebookshop.co.uk
www.japancentre.com
Origami and Japanese handmade paper supplier.

London Graphic Centre
16/18 Shelton Street
Covent Garden
London WC2H 9JL
tel: 020 7759 4500
fax: 020 7759 4585
www.londongraphics.co.uk
Stationery, graphic and fine art retailer.

Paper2Go
PO Box 314
Hull HU2 0WZ
tel: 0870 129 8516
fax: 0870 129 8517
www.paper2go.co.uk
Coloured and textured paper and card, metallic paper and translucent paper supplier.

The Paper Warehouse
Grosvenor House Papers Ltd
Westmorland Business Park
Kendal LA9 6NP
tel: 01539 726161
email: info@ghpkendal.co.uk
www.ghpkendal.co.uk
General craft retailer of a wide range of paper craft supplies including punches and peel-offs.

Europe

Ideal Home Range
email: info@ihr-online.de
www.idealhomerange.com
Paper manufacture. Contact for local stockists.

Kars Creative Wholesale
Industrieweg 27
Industrieterrein 'De Heuning'
Postbus 97
4050 EB Ochten
The Netherlands
tel: +31 (0) 344 642864
fax: +31 (0) 344 643509
email: info@kars.nl
www.kars.nl
Wholesaler of a vast range of craft materials. Contact for local stockists.

USA

Fascinating Folds
PO Box 10070
Glendale
AZ 85318
www.fascinating-folds.com
An extensive supplier of reference materials for paper art and crafts.

Nasco Arts and Crafts
4825 Stoddard Road
Modesto
CA 95397 - 3837
email: custserv@eNASCO.com
www.nascofa.com
Carries a comprehensive selection of arts and craft materials.

Stamporium
1016 - 50th PL. W.
Mukilteo
Washington WE 98275
www.stamporium.com
Offers new and exciting paper-craft products imported from the Netherlands.

Twinrocker Handmade Paper
100 East 3rd Street
Brookston
IN 47923
www.twinrocker.com
Supplier of handmade paper and an importer of decorative papers.

Australia

Glitzy Bits
www.glizybits.com.au
An online shop for handcrafted embellishments and punches.

Japanese Paper and Origami Supplies
PO BOX 558
Summer Hill
NSW 2130
email: sales@origami.com.au
www.origami.com.au
Supplier of Japanese handmade paper and origami products.

Scrap Booking Corner
PO Box 339
Helensburgh
NSW 2508
email: contactus@scrapbookingcorner.com.au
www.scrapbookingcorner.com.au
Stockist of stickers, papers, punches and deckle-edged scissors.

Paperfolding Societies

The following organizations offer a broad range of origami books, private publications on the various aspects of paperfolding, packaged origami paper and information on the many international origami associations. They also hold regular meetings and yearly conventions that may include practical classes and exhibitions of the latest creations. They welcome folding enthusiasts of any age or level.

The Membership Secretary
British Origami Society
2A The Chestnuts
Countesthorpe
Leicestershire LE8 5TL
www.britishorigami.org.uk

The Envelope and Letterfold Association
PO Box 16181
London NW1
email: heide.karst@t-online.de

O.U.S.A. Center of America
15 West 77th Street
New York
New York 10024-5192
USA
www.origami-usa.org

The Australian Origami Society
www.freewebs.com/perthorigami

Visit Joseph Wu's origami website at:
www.origami.vancouver.bc.ca

About the Authors

Steve Biddle is an author, entertainer and origami expert. He has studied in Japan with the top Japanese origami masters where he acquired a deeper knowledge of a subject that has always fascinated him. He is also a member of the most famous magical society in the world, The Magic Circle.

Megumi Biddle is a graphic artist, designer and illustrator with a long-standing interest in paper crafts and doll-making. At the 1985 All Japan Handcraft Art Society's exhibition, held in the Tokyo Art Museum, she received the society's top debut award for developing her own unique style of doll-making. She is also a highly skilled silhouette artist and has cut out the profiles of many well-known celebrities. Steve and Megumi have performed their 'Paper Magic' act at a variety of functions and taken their act across the world, having performed in Europe, Australia, the United States and Japan. They have appeared on many television programmes, such as *Blue Peter* and *The Generation Game* in the UK. Together they have designed items for television, films and advertising campaigns and produced many highly successful craft and picture books both for children and adults. They live on the south coast of England with, Hana, their Japanese Akita dog.

Acknowledgments

We would like to thank the following: John Cunliffe for his assistance with the index. For reviewing the text, Doreen and Caroline Montgomery. A special thank you to Ian and Donna Carter and their family for testing the project instructions. For sharing their origami creations with us our deepest thanks go to: Shōko Aoyagi, Tomoko Fuse, Zsuzsanna Kricskovics, Hiroshi Kumasaka and Makoto Yamaguchi. Finally, we would like to express our gratitude to the David & Charles editorial and design teams.

Index